DATE DUE			
NOV 2 '84			
Sep 30 '85			
NOV 10 1986			

MAN
AND THE SACRED

MAN
AND THE SACRED

By Roger Caillois

Translated by Meyer Barash

GREENWOOD PRESS, PUBLISHERS
WESTPORT, CONNECTICUT

Library of Congress Cataloging in Publication Data

Caillois, Roger, 1913-
  Man and the sacred.

  Translation of L'homme et le sacré.
  Reprint of the ed. published by Free Press of Glencoe,
Ill.
  Bibliography: p.
  Includes index.
  1. Religion. 2. Religion and sociology. 3. Rites
and ceremonies. I. Title.
[BL48.C2813 1980]   306'.6   79-8709
ISBN 0-313-22196-0 lib. bdg.

Published as *L'homme et le sacré,* to which have been added three Appendices on Sex, Play, and War as related to the Sacred (Gallimard, 2d ed., 1950).

Reprinted in 1980 by Greenwood Press,
a division of Congressional Information Service, Inc.
51 Riverside Avenue, Westport, Connecticut 06880

Printed in the United States of America

10 9 8 7 6 5 4 3 2 1

CONTENTS

TRANSLATOR'S INTRODUCTION

Roger Caillois, French sociologist, literary critic, and editor of *Diogenes*, is a writer whose name and work should become better known in the English-speaking world. Not only has he written with originality and distinction in the sociology of religion, but in addition he has published extensively in such areas as comparative mythology, the sociology of the novel, and even the evolution of the detective story. In an age of extreme specialism and empiricism, his works are a continuous proof of the viability of the European tradition of scholarship, representing as they do an impressive mastery of the humanities as well as the social sciences.

Caillois comes by his interest in the sociology of religion through the direct inspiration and teaching of such masters as Durkheim and Mauss, and hàs contributed to the future training of scholars in this field by founding the *Collège de Sociologie pour l'Étude du Sacré* at the University of Beauvais. It was with the thought that students on both sides of the Atlantic would be benefited by wider dissemination of his ideas that this translation was undertaken.

The first edition of *L'homme et le sacré* was published in 1939, by Presses Universitaires de France and its success prompted Caillois to issue a revised and expanded version in 1946 through Gallimard. While Durkheim, Mauss, Lévy-Bruhl, and other important figures in the development of French sociology had been concerned with the role of the sacred in society, it remained for Caillois to link provocatively the concept of the sacred with the concept of the festival and to trace the detailed consequences of this union both analytically and comparatively. Throughout the study, numerous illustrations in support of his argument are drawn from such ethnographic classics as those of Spencer and Gillen, Lévy-Bruhl, Mauss, and Granet.

Caillois develops his thesis approximately as follows. He uses as his point of departure the sacred—profane dichotomy. The domain of the sacred, unlike that of the profane, is one of fear and hope, an aura rather than a state, surrounded by mystery, evanescent in its qualities, a powerful and dangerous force in man's life. Furthermore, it is susceptible to dilution, dissipation, or debasement by the profane. There are consecration and deconsecration rites designed to control its impact, and taboos are created in order to protect the *ordo mundi*, the universal order of both nature and society. The sphere of the profane is that of common usage, and that of the sacred is what is forbidden. Sacrifice, asceticism, offerings, and related rituals define man's behavior toward the sacred.

In the four subsequent essays, Caillois stresses the ambiguity of the sacred, the sacred as respect—clarifying the avoidance mechanisms involved in taboos, the sacred as transgression—illustrating the cathartic function of the festival, and lastly, the persistance of the sacred through the life cycle of the individual in all the passage rites that he must celebrate. Throughout the study, the relationship between the rituals described and the social cohesion of the group is stressed.

In the first appendix on *Sex and the Sacred,* Caillois draws upon Junod's classic monograph on the Thonga to further document his thesis on the role of the sacred. His second appendix, *Play and the Sacred,* is possibly the best critique yet published of J. Huizinga's *Homo Ludens,* wherein Caillois argues cogently against completely identifying play and the sacred. In the last appendix, *War and the Sacred,* he makes a persuasive analogy between the functional significance of war in modern society and the festival in primitive society.

However, Caillois' approach serves to underline the differences between European and American canons of scholarship. The book is replete with fertile generalizations, intuitive insights, and quick analogies, any of which could be the basis for a monograph in itself. On the other hand, by contemporary American standards, the author is often careless in documentation and overly reliant on reinterpreting the classics for illustrative purposes; he almost completely ignores the more recent sociological and anthropological literature.

For example, Caillois relies almost exclusively, upon the comparative method, which has fallen into a certain degree of disrepute. (This was due to the tendency of traditional writers to be selective to a degree almost to the point of oversimplification and generalization, unjustified by the empirical materials.) More careful analysis of the data on Eskimo, Australian, New Caledonian, and Chinese society—based on the most recent field investigations—would seem warranted. Furthermore, it is hoped that, in subsequent inquiries on this theme, Caillois' analysis might gain in conceptual rigor through utilizing Howard Becker's sacred-secular typology and R. K. Merton's analysis in terms of manifest and latent functions.

Nevertheless, it is believed that the major value of this work lies in its bold hypotheses, classical scholarship, and brilliant insights—all of which should have a salutary effect upon current inquiries into the sociology of religion.

It should be noted parenthetically, that on the frequent occasions when special problems of transliterating place-names, tribes, moieties, clans, and terms designating ceremonies occurred, changes in spelling, consistent with current anthropological usage had to be made. In disputed cases, Robert F. Spencer's *An Ethno-Atlas* (Dubuque, Iowa: William C. Brown Company, 1956) was often helpful. But the translator's greatest debt is to his colleague Dr. Arnold Pilling, whose prodigious knowledge of the relevant anthropological literature made it possible to track down many an obscure textual reference. Gratitude must also be expressed to the secretarial staff of the Department of Sociology and Anthropology for undertaking the burden of typing a difficult manuscript despite the pressure of numerous other clerical duties. Lastly, special thanks must go to Messrs. Jeremiah Kaplan and John Bettin of the Free Press of Glencoe, Illinois, for sponsoring the translation, and furnishing both financial and editorial assistance for the venture.

Meyer Barash
Wayne State University
Detroit, Michigan

PREFACE TO

THE SECOND EDITION

The first edition of this work appeared in 1939. I had to reduce its length somewhat in order to conform to the space limitations of the series in which it was to be published. In this edition, I have presented the entire text. For Chapter II, where I introduce certain new developments, I have in large part utilized the text of a study originally written for *L'Histoire générale des Religions*,[1] which, because of the war, was not published until 1948. The entire text of Chapter III was originally published in *Revue d'Histoire des Religions*[2] and is reprinted as is, except for references, in this edition.

In the remaining chapters, only nominal changes have been made. Only those that alter the preceding text are cited in footnotes.

The first of the three appendices, "Sex and the Sacred," is already part of the Spanish translation of this book.[3] The second, "Play and the Sacred," which criticizes the theories advanced by J. Huizinga in his book *Homo Ludens*, was published March, 1946, in the review, *Confluances*.[4] Since then, M. Benveniste has published a definitive study on the same subject[5] that corroborates and completes my essay. I made reference to the major points of his study in the footnotes. Finally, the third appendix, "War and the Sacred," tries to resolve a problem posed at the end of Chapter IV, viz., what corresponds to the holiday, in modern societies? At first, I thought of a vacation, but it is clear that the characteristics of the holiday and the vacation, far from being identical, are on the contrary significantly opposed. It is war that corresponds to the holiday. I can include in this book only a small part of the documentation I have gathered that permits one to best perceive the functional similarity of the two social paroxysms. I am hoping for an opportunity to devote a special work to the evolution of modern war and to the sentiments of horror and exaltation it generally stimulates. In this way, I hope to show in greater detail at what point, in keeping with war's role as all-pervasive phenomenon of contemporary societies, it revives for its advantage the beliefs and the behavior that are ordinarily appropriate to sacred places.

Some works appearing since 1939 make important contributions to the study of the issues treated in the present volume. I have added them to the topical bibliography at the back of the book. I have had the satisfaction of finding in them valuable confirmation for the propositions that I defended on the system of taboos and exchange, that is to say, on the economy of the sacred in "primitive" societies. In particular, it concerns the supposed ban on incest, in the negative sense. Second, it concerns the rule that renders intermarriage between complementary groups obligatory.

This book has even received more direct verification. In Latin America, particularly for a whole week at the carnivals in Rio de Janeiro and Veracruz, the entire population of the city and its environs intermingles, sings, dances, moves about and makes a din—in almost ceaseless excitement. I have been able to prove that my description of the holiday, far from being fanciful, corresponds in essence to living and observable facts—even though visibly in decline because of the pressures of contemporary urban life.

So, thanks to this varied encouragement, I am taking the risks, not too rashly, of producing a second edition, which contains more elaboration than changes.

                                            November, 1949

INTRODUCTION

Basically, with regard to the sacred in general, the only thing that can be validly asserted is contained in the very definition of the term—that it is opposed to the profane. As soon as one attempts to specify the nature and conditions of this opposition, one comes up against serious obstacles. Elementary as it may be, no formula is applicable to the labyrinthian complexity of the facts. Examined in a certain perspective, the sacred finds itself rudely contradicted by a mass of facts arranged in baffling sequence. Should one begin with a multitude of monographs on the relationship of the sacred to the profane in each society? This would be the work of several lifetimes, if the research includes a sufficient number of cases. If the investigation is incomplete, there is the danger of hasty and oversimplified generalization. Given these limitations, I resigned myself to describing types of relationships. This lacked prudence, perhaps, but was more honest. The analytical aspect of this work is doubtless overstressed. I have been ambitious by necessity. Being unable to attack the study of the inexhaustible morphology of the sacred, I have tried to write its syntax.

It is now necessary to spell out, while admitting without evasion, the fallacious and crude aspects of such a venture. The descriptions pertain to precise facts that were selected as the best substantiated and most characteristic but were taken out of their context, out of the totality of beliefs and behavior of which they are part and which gives them meaning. They are not much more than abstractions, losing most of their concrete value. Also, the conclusions are only valid for the typicality of facts, to which no concrete fact exactly corresponds. In a way, they constitute statements of rules that never wholly apply, of rules, in a word, that only allow exceptions. For example, there is no holiday, to be sure, that can be wholly explained by the theory I have outlined of the holiday as such. Each fulfils a precise function in a specific situation. Nevertheless, I do not believe that the theory is useless. Even though it does not furnish us with the meaning of the variables, at least the theory attempts to isolate the constant. I have never described the locks or the keys fitting exactly into the locks. I have only proposed a master-key. This latter is not without inconvenience, and in no way precludes (it is obvious) resorting in case of need to a good key, that is to say, to examine the question in and of itself.

Rudolf Otto is the author of a solid work expanding the "subjective" side of the subject, i.e., treating the sacred sentiments. The sacred is analyzed therein from a psychological viewpoint, in almost introspective fashion and almost exclusively in terms of the forms that it has taken in the great universalistic religions. I have deemed it possible, under these circumstances, to omit making a frontal assault upon this aspect of the problem while reserving the right, nevertheless, to refer to it whenever it appeared useful to me to do so. For the rest, I have followed with care the writings of the French school of sociology. I trust that I have not been too faithless to them in trying to co-ordinate their conclusions. The reader will observe, as he proceeds, all that this work owes to the syntheses that do honor to such personages as Durkheim, Hubert and Hertz, just as those of Mauss, Granet, and Dumézil continue to guide me so well. No one other than Marcel Mauss should have been designated to write a book on the sacred. Everyone is convinced that this book would have been for a long time *the* book on the sacred. I cannot take his place in this task without peril and anxiety. At least, I can find some relief from my uneasiness in the fact that my work has profited not only from Mauss's published works, but even more from extraordinary, and positive suggestions with which, in the course of a simple conversation, he can stimulate the labors of those who seek his counsel. In particular, if in this work a favored place is given to the concept of the *ordo rerum,* credit for this belongs to Mauss alone. It is impossible for me to indicate precisely my indebtedness to Georges Dumézil. So greatly do I appreciate him that if I tried to specify it, I would wrong the mentor who, in the history of religions, has directed me from the very first steps, and still more would I wrong the friend whose suggestions and guidance have contributed so much to this little volume. Finally, I have to express my gratitude to Georges Bataille. It seems to me that with this subject there was established between us a kind of intellectual osmosis, which, on my part, does not permit me to distinguish with certainty, after so many discussions, his contribution from mine, in the work that we pursued in common.

I do not believe it possible to avoid posing the metaphysical issue. The problem of the sacred seems to me to concern something in man that is profound and basic. Doubtless, I have gone beyond the limits of positive knowledge, further than is permissable. Perhaps some would have found this work incomplete without such imprudence. I admit sharing their sentiment. Yet the others very much desire not to hold me rigorously to what they gladly consider a deviation. Thus they are satisfied to ignore it. I do not think that the last ten pages of a book are sufficient to discredit the pages preceding them, when the latter have been composed with no mental reservations, with objectivity the sole concern, entirely independent of a conclusion that they lead toward only by the power of circumstances.

March, 1939

MAN
AND THE SACRED

Chapter I—GENERAL INTERRELATIONSHIPS OF THE SACRED AND THE PROFANE

EVERY RELIGIOUS CONCEPTION OF THE UNIVERSE IMPLIES A distinction between the sacred and the profane and is opposed to the world in which the believer freely attends to his business and engages in activity heedless of his salvation. The domain of the sacred is one in which he is paralyzed in turn by fear and by hope—a world in which, as at the edge of an abyss, the least misstep, the least movement can doom him irrevocably. To be sure, such a distinction is not always sufficient to define the phenomenon of religion, but at least it supplies a touchstone enabling us to recognize it with greater certainty. In effect, whatever definition is proposed for religion, it is remarkable how this opposition between the sacred and the profane is involved in it, even though not coinciding with it purely and simply. For a long time now, by logical inference or direct verification, it has been observed that religious man is, above all, one for whom two complimentary universes exist—one, in which he can act without anxiety or trepidation, but in which his actions only involve his superficial self; the other, in which a feeling of deep dependency controls, contains, and directs each of his drives, and to which he is committed unreservedly. These two worlds, the sacred and the profane, are rigorously defined only in relation to each other. They are mutually exclusive and contradictory. It is useless to try eliminating this contradiction. This opposition appears to be a genuinely intuitive concept. We can describe it, analyze it into its elements, and theorize about it. But it is no more within the power of abstract language to define its unique quality than to define a sensation. Thus the sacred seems like a category of feeling. In truth, that is the level on which religious attitudes exist and which gives them their special character. A feeling of special reverence imbues the believer, which fortifies his faith against critical inquiry, makes it immune to discussion, and places it outside and beyond reason.

"It is the basic idea of religion," writes H. Hubert. "Myths and dogmas characteristically comprise its content, ritual reflects its qualities, religious ethics derives from it, priesthoods embody it, sanctuaries, holy places and religious monuments enshrine it and enroot it. Religion is the administration of the sacred."

We couldn't stress more forcefully the points at which the experience of the sacred animates all the various manifestations of the religious way of life. This latter is, in effect, the sum total of man's relationships with the sacred. Creeds reveal and assure permanence to these relationships. Rites are the means of proving them in practice.

MAJOR CHARACTERISTICS OF THE SACRED

The sacred is related as a common property, solid or ephemeral, to certain objects (the instruments of the cult), to certain beings (kings, priests), to certain places (temple, church, mountain peak), to certain times (Sunday, Easter, Christmas, etc.). There is nothing that cannot become its resting place and thus clothe it in the eyes of the individual or the group with an unequaled prestige. The sacred is not something that can be taken away. It is a quality that things do not possess in themselves—a mysterious aura that has been added to things. "The bird which flies," a Dakota Indian explained to Miss Fletcher, "stops to build his nest. Man, who walks, stops where he pleases. Thus it is with divinity; the sun is one place where it has lodged, trees and animals are others. That is why we pray to them, for we reach the place where the sacred has stopped, and receive its succor and blessing."

The sacred being, the consecrated object, can in no way be modified in its appearance. Nevertheless, it is transformed in moving from person to person. From this moment on, the manner of its movement undergoes a parallel modification. It is no longer possible to partake of it freely. It stimulates feelings of terror and veneration; it becomes "taboo." Contact with it becomes dangerous. Automatic and immediate punishment would strike the imprudent one, as surely as flame burns the hand that touches it. The sacred is always more or less "what one cannot approach without dying."

As for the profane, one must, for reasons of self-interest, guard against a familiarity as deadly in its speed and its effects as the contagion of the sacred is crushing. The force that man or the holy contains is always ready to escape, to evaporate like a liquid, to discharge like electricity. It is no less necessary to protect the sacred from any taint of the profane. The profane, in effect, alters its essence, causes it to lose its unique quality—the void created by the impression of the formidible and fleeting power it contains. That is why we are careful to remove from a sacred place all that pertains to the profane world. Only the priest penetrates into the holy of holies. In Australia, the place where sacred objects or *churingas* are kept is not known by all. In the mysteries of the cult for which these objects are sacred instruments, the profane are kept ignorant of their hiding place. They only know its approximate site, and if they approach its vicinity, they have to make a great detour to avoid discovering it by chance. Among the Maori, if a woman enters the area in which a sacred boat is being built, the seaworthiness of the boat is affected and it cannot be launched. The presence of a profane being serves to remove the divine blessing. A woman who walks into a sacred place destroys its sanctity.

Without doubt, the profane, in relationship to the sacred, simply endows it with negative properties. The profane, in comparison, seems as poor and bereft of existence as nothingness is to being. But as R. Hertz expresses it so aptly, it is a *néant actif* that debases, degrades, and destroys the substance in terms of which it is defined. Thus it happens that watertight compartments separate the sacred from the profane. Any contact between them is fatal. "The two categories," writes Durkheim, "cannot be brought together without thereby losing their unique characteristics." On the other hand, they are both necessary for the evolution of life—one, as the environment within which life unfolds; the other, as the inexhaustible source that creates, sustains, and renews it.

THE SACRED, SOURCE OF SUCCESS

It is from the sacred, in effect, that the believer expects all succor and success. The reverence in which he holds the sacred is composed equally of terror and confidence. The calamities that menace and victimize him, the prosperity that he desires or gains, is attributed by him to some principle that he strives to control or constrain. It is of little importance what he imagines the supreme origin of grace or his ordeals to be—the universal and omnipotent God of the monotheistic religions; protective divinities of cities; spirits of the dead; an animistic power that gives each object its appropriate function, that makes boats rapid, weapons lethal, and food nourishing. As complex or simple as one can imagine, religion implies the recognition of this force with which man must reckon. All that seems to him to contain it appears sacred, terrible, and precious. On the other hand, he regards everything from which the sacred is absent as no doubt harmless, but powerless and unalluring. One can have only disdain for the profane, while the sacred inspires a kind of fascination. At the same time, it constitutes the supreme temptation and the greatest of dangers. Dreadful, it commands caution, and desirable, it invites rashness.

Thus, in its basic form, the sacred represents a dangerous force, incomprehensible, intractable but eminently efficacious. For the one who decides to have recourse to it, the problem consists of capturing and utilizing it in his best interest, while at the same time protecting himself against the risks inherent in using a force so difficult to control. The more important the goal pursued, the more is the intervention of the sacred necessary, and the more perilous is preparation for it. The sacred cannot be subdued, diluted, or divided. It is indivisible and always a totality wherever it is found. In each bit of the consecrated wafer, the divinity of Christ, is present in its entirety, for the smallest fragment of a relic possesses all the power of the total relic. The profane person must be careful in his desire to appropriate this power and must take proper precautions. The infidel who lays his hand upon the tabernacle sees it wither and crumble into dust. An unprepared individual cannot bear such a transformation of energy. The substance of the sacrilege becomes turgid, its branches diffuse and twist, its flesh decomposes, it soon dies of languor or convulsions. That is why, in some tribes, one must avoid touching the person of the chief when it is deemed sacred. The clothes the chief wears, the dish from which he eats, and his uneaten food are destroyed—burnt or buried. No one, except his own children who share his sanctity, dares to pick up a feather or turban that falls from the chief's head lest illness or death result.

THE FUNCTION OF RITUAL AND TABOOS

On the one hand, the contagiousness of the sacred causes it to spread instantaneously to the profane, and thus to risk destroying and dissipating itself uselessly. On the other hand, the profane always needs the sacred, is always pressed to possess it avidly, and thus to risk degrading the sacred or being annihilated by it. Their reciprocal relationships, therefore, have to be strictly regulated. This is precisely the function of ritual. First, the positive function of ritual is to transform the nature of the profane or the sacred according to the needs of the society. Second, the negative function of ritual is, on the contrary, to keep the profane and the sacred as they are, lest they destroy each other by coming into improper contact. The former comprise *consecration* rites, which initiate people and things into the world of the sacred, and *deconsecration* or expiation rites, which, conversely, make persons or things pure or impure in the profane world. These rites establish and assure the ins and outs indispensable to the two worlds. Prohibitions, on the contrary, raise an equally indispensable barrier between the sacred and the profane, which separates them but saves them from catastrophe. These prohibitions are ordinarily designated by the Polynesian term *taboo*. "We use this word," writes Durkheim, "for a category of ritualistic interdictions which have the effect of preventing the dangerous results of magical contagion, by avoiding any contact with an object or class of objects in which a supernatural principle is supposed to reside, and of others which do not have this property, or not to the same degree."

The taboo is like a categorical imperative. It always involves forbidding, never sanctioning. It is not justified by any moral consideration. One must not infringe upon it, for the sole and unique reason that it is the law, and it absolutely defines what is and is not permitted. It is destined to maintain the integration of organized society and, at the same time, the health and morale of the individual who complies. It keeps one man from dying and another from reverting to the chaotic and fluid stage, formless and vague, of which he was part before divine beings or ancestral heroes arrived to bring him order, dimensions, stability, and regularity. In the primordial state of license, taboos did not exist. His ancestors, in instituting them, established the proper order and functioning of the universe. They determined, once and for all, the relationships between men and things, between men and their Gods. They outlined the boundaries of the sacred and the profane and defined the limits of the allowable and the forbidden. In Polynesian, the opposite of *taboo* is "free" *noa. Noa* is that which is allowable, without questioning the order of the universe, without unleashing misfortune and calamity, and that which entails no inordinate or irremediable consequences. On the other hand, an act is *taboo* that cannot be performed without attacking the universal order of both nature and society. Each transgression upsets the entire order.

The earth may not be able to yield a harvest; the beasts of creation are rendered sterile; the stars can no longer follow their course; illness and death ravage the countryside. The culprit does not endanger merely his own person. The trouble that he has caused in the world brings the contamination nearer and nearer until it mars the wholeness of the universe, unless the evil loses its violence gradually as it spreads, or unless means have been provided and immediately applied to check or alleviate it.

In summary, according to this brief preliminary description, the sphere of the profane appears to be that of *common usage*, that of acts which do not require precautions and which stay in the oft narrow space left to man in which he may act without constraint. The world of the sacred, on the contrary, appears to be that of the dangerous or of the forbidden. The individual cannot approach it without unleashing forces of which he is not the master and against which his weakness makes him helpless. However, without their assistance, his desires are doomed to frustration. In these forces resides the source of all success, power, luck. But when invoking them, one dreads becoming their first victim.

THE ORDER OF THE UNIVERSE

This ambiguous status of the sacred defines in basic terms the manner in which man perceives it. The study of the sacred from a subjective point of view has to rest upon this ambiguity. Yet it is necessary, in addition, to investigate what follows objectively from the restrictions imposed upon the individual, which he believes himself obligated to observe. We have seen that these prohibitions were supposed to contribute to the maintenance of the cosmic order. In effect, the word referring to the violation of these prohibitions is usually derived from a term that is the negative of that which defines the universal law. This illustrates the strict relationship between the two concepts. To the latin *fas* is opposed the *nefas*, which comprises all that touches upon the order of the universe, of divine law, and is forbidden by it. The Greek *thémis*, which equally assures the order of the universe, connotes not so much the moral notion of justice as that of regularity, indispensable to the proper functioning of the universe and, equally, a characteristic or consequence of it. Taboos are introduced by the formula *ou thémis,* which signifies nothing else than the inconsistency of the prohibited act with the sacred prescriptions keeping the world orderly and stable. Again, opposed to the Indo-Iranian *rta,* the *an-rta* designates everything that contradicts the universal order. When Yamî asks his twin brother to engage in incest, the latter refuses, citing the traditional law, "What we have never done, how can we now do? How can we practice *an-rta,* when we preach *rta?*" Neither must violate the edicts of the cosmic code. When Indra was found guilty of the murder of Vrtra, of the Brahman caste, the burden of his transgression, however justifiable, deprives him of his power. He must flee to the end of the earth and hide in a reed while the universe is left prey to catastrophe. "Whoever follows the *rta* finds the path easy and free of brambles," but conversely, he who deviates from the beaten path, from the primordial standard, brings to pass incalculable and far reaching evils. Xerxes, who threw a bridge of boats upon the Bosphorus and caused rough seas, brought about the defeat of his army and led it to disaster. In China, if the sovereign or his spouse transgresses the laws, the sun or the moon goes into eclipse.

THE HAZARDS OF INTERMIXTURE

The natural order is a continuation of the social order and reflects it. Both are connected. What troubles one disturbs the other. A crime of *lèse-majesté* is like an act against nature, equally injurious to the proper functioning of the universe. In the same way, to mix the two is a dangerous operation which may result in confusion and disorder, which particularly risks confounding the properties that should be kept separate if their special virtues are to be preserved. That is why most of the taboos in force in so-called primitive societies are primarily mixed taboos. It is recognized that direct or indirect contact, simultaneous presence in a very confined area, already constitute intermingling. These are dreaded when they tend, for example, to adhere to objects that, in any way, by contagion or naturally, seem to belong to one or the other sex. Thus it is that, in some tribes, the implements of the male cannot be placed next to those of the female, nor can their respective crops be stored under the same roof. Again, one is afraid to mix what pertains to different seasons. Among the Eskimo, walrus hides taken from a Winter animal must not be in contact with reindeer skins, taken from a Summer animal, just as walrus and reindeer meat may not be side by side, even in the stomachs of those who eat it.

Variations are innumerable. All natural oppositions, as those of the sexes or the seasons, can give birth to rules capable of maintaining the integrity of the principles that other wise would be contradicted. The oppositions of social origin, as those of various groupings that compose the tribe, likewise institute taboos that prevent any evil contamination of their unique properties. Australian tribes are divided into two moieties.[6] The platform on which a corpse is exposed must be built exclusively with the type of wood belonging to its own moiety. On the other hand, in order to hunt an animal under the jurisdiction of a given moiety it is necessary to use weapons made of wood belonging to the other moiety. This is because the intermixture is not considered by their religion as a kind of chemical operation with definite and, in any case, purely material consequences. It involves the very essence of the matter. It is disturbed and altered, an impurity is introduced, in other words, a contagious focus of infection, that must be destroyed, eliminated, or isolated without delay.

The properties of objects are contagious. They change, reverse, combine, and corrupt each other if too great a proximity permits them to interact. The order of the universe is offended to that degree. Furthermore, it is theoretically necessary to preserve it, to prevent any mixing capable of compromising this order. In proceeding with this analysis, precautions for mitigating the effects of intermixture will be described.

THE NATURE OF SACRIFICE

In another respect, the individual desires to succeed in his enterprises, or to acquire those virtues that will enable him to succeed, and prevent the misfortunes lying in wait for him or the punishment that he deserves for his shortcomings. His whole society, city, or tribe finds itself in the same situation. If war is necessary, he seeks victory and fears defeat. If he enjoys prosperity, he desires to keep it forever; he is preoccupied with avoiding the ruin that he anticipates with foreboding. There are, however, favors that the individual or state have to obtain from the Gods, personal or impersonal powers upon which the order of the world is believed to depend. Yet the supplicant can imagine nothing better, in order to control the Gods and have them yield to him, than to take the initiative by making them a gift or a *sacrifice,* that is by consecrating, by presenting at his expense to the domain of the sacred, something that belongs to him and that he gives up, something of which he has free disposition and to which he renounces every right. The sacred powers that cannot refuse this usurious gift become the debtors of the donor, are bound by what they have received, and to be left in peace, have to grant what he is asking of them—material advantage, strength, or remission of punishment. The order of the universe is thus re-established. Through sacrifice, the believer becomes a creditor; he expects the powers that he venerates to pay off the debts that they have contracted on his account by granting his desires. Having done this, they furnish the response that all unilateral acts require and restore the balance that the supplicant's selfish generosity has disturbed, to his profit.

ASCETICISM AND OFFERINGS

The principle behind both asceticism and offerings is similar for every act by which one voluntarily deprives oneself of a pleasure or an advantage. In effect, it is known that asceticism is indeed the road to power. The ascetic keeps voluntarily within the realm of legal or material possibility and is careful to act in ways that the laws or his powers permit. He maintains in this way a certain latitude, always large, between what he can do, in law as well as in fact, and that with which he must be content. That is why each renunciation redounds to his credit in the mythical world and assures him an equal latitude in supernatural possibilities. He acquires, by the impossible and the forbidden, a *beyond* reserved for him alone and corresponding exactly to the *here and now* of the possible and the permitted that he had abandoned. But this exchange constitutes the most profitable of investments, for what he disdained in the profane he recovers in the sacred. The ascetic, who augments his powers to the degree that he diminishes his pleasures, transcends mankind, approaches the Gods, and rapidly becomes their peer. It is, moreover, to his profit that the balance should be disturbed. The Gods dread having to pay dearly for so many mortifications, and soon have to lead him into all manner of temptations in order to deprive him of a power capable of upsetting theirs. This theme recurs repeatedly in mythology.

In the same way, the victim that is offered up and destroyed by sacrifice represents a deprivation imposed upon oneself in the hope of a larger reward. Similarly, we torment ourselves in order to pay in advance for the happiness we are seeking from the Gods. The Gros Ventre Indians actually engage in self-torture on the eve of a military expedition. The Hupa bathe in icy rivers in order to assure the success of their enterprises. A New Guinea tribe combats female sterility by making incisions on their upper thighs. Among the Arunta and the Warramunga, men and women wound their arms with flaming sticks so as to become skillful at lighting the sacred fire. Circumcision and subcision are practiced in order to make the individual ready for marriage, to increase his potency and reproductive power, or simply to immunize his sexual organs against the mysterious perils that conjugal relations may visit upon him. Thus, through appropriate suffering he always raises the price of the advantage that he is seeking. Equally, he is saved from an evil that he dreads, while practicing self-denial with good grace. Polycrates throws his ring into the sea in order to avert the catastrophe that the very abundance of his good fortune makes him dread. In other places, the death of a parent threatens the lives of one's family. The defilement of death can reach them next and cause them to perish. Often, they save themselves from death by mutilating their bodies, generally by cutting off a finger. Thus, the part is sacrificed in order to save the whole.

THE RITUAL OF THE FIRST-FRUITS[7]

The consecration of the first-fruits seems to be based on the same psychology. This time, the part is sacrificed not to save but to acquire the whole. In fact, each beginning poses a delicate problem. An equilibrium is broken—a new element had been added that must be introduced into the order of the universe with least disturbance. That is why the first of a series is regarded as dangerous. One dare not put it in common use. It belongs by right to the divine. It is consecrated by the very fact that it is first, that it inaugurates a new order of things, that it is the cause of change. When the crop is grown, it must be freed before it can be harvested. The first and fattest ears of corn in the harvest, the first and most beautiful fruit of the orchard, the first and biggest vegetables of the garden are reserved for the Gods. Especially holy people are charged with absorbing the terrible force that the first-fruits conceal in their newness. Thus, among the Zulus, the king or priest is the first to taste new produce, then each of his assistants takes a mouthful, and the latter can then dispose of it as they please for the rest of the year.

The Ancient Hebrews did not reap for themselves the fruits of the trees they had planted until the fifth year. The fruit of the first three years was deemed impure, and the fourth was dedicated to God. In the same way, they sacrificed the first-born of domestic animals. Even man himself was not exempted from this rule. He often had to offer up his first son, as Abraham did Isaac, or at least dedicate him to the divine cult. The first-born represents the Gods' share. By his consecration he atones for the trouble that his coming into the world has caused to its order. At the same time, he redeems his brothers, assures them a free and profane existence, and permits them unqualifiedly to belong to their parents.

Every change in status requires, in the same way, an offering of first-fruits, the purpose of which is to absorb the dangers inherent in such change. Before marriage, in some cultures, the girl yields the symbolic first-fruits of her virginity to a river or a God. Among people where defloration prior to marriage has been long practiced, the bride must at the time of her marriage have had relationships with at least one other man before having them with her husband. This is in order to save her husband from the danger that the embrace of a married woman connotes—that is, of a person who inaugurates a new social status and a new kind of existence.

To take possession of a newly constructed edifice involves analogous risks. A sacrificial dance often frees the ground for habitation. Sometimes, the sorcerer removes the soul from the one who is going to enter the new house and puts it in a place where it will be safe. He restores it to its owner after he has crossed the formidable line, until then inviolate, that the threshold of the new dwelling represents. We know the oft told tory, according to which the devil helps build a church or bridge on condition that he take possession of the soul of the first one who enters there. Examples of this are infinitely varied, but they all demonstrate the absolute danger attached to every beginning and the necessity of partial consecration that can integrate into the order of things the element that has been introduced.

THE STUDY OF THE SACRED

Moreover, it is never a question of a makeshift device. The healing of each wound leaves a scar. The restoration of the disturbed order does not give back its primitive stability or its original purity. Life persists, thanks to its dynamic quality, only by continuous regeneration, which is tiring for the organism and which forces it to a ceaseless assimilation of new matter. Such are rites of atonement, the solemn elimination of impurities, various cleansing and purging practices restoring the order of the universe, which is under constant attack. These can never restore the virtue of innocence, but rather a prudent state of health never again triumphant and free from care as it was prior to the illness. It is impossible "that the grain under the millstone can ever be replaced in the ear of corn," "that the awkward shoot or the tender nerve penetrate the surface and ever again break through."

To protect nature and society from the inevitable aging process that would lead it to ruin, it is important to take the precaution of periodically rejuvenating and regenerating it. This obligation opens a new chapter in the study of the sacred. It will not suffice to describe the functioning of the order of the world, to note that the powers of the sacred are kept for good or for evil, aiding respectively in the cohesion or precipitating the dissolution of the universal order. It will be necessary, in addition, to indicate the way in which man labors to maintain this order, and the efforts he exerts to renew it when he sees it crumbling and near collapse. But, before investigating how society acquits itself of this double task, before beginning to outline a sociology of the sacred, perhaps it is necessary to isolate several constants in man's attitude toward the sacred, in the conception he has of the prodigious forces before which he bows, from which he protects himself, and which he wishes to possess at the same time. Without a doubt, to the degree that each person is a member of a society, the fact of the sacred gains its true significance to the same degree. But it is not merely the individual's mind that is fascinated by the sacred, but all of his being. The value of the sacred is obvious, and must be adapted to his needs.

So too, without wishing to analyze in detail the feelings that it stimulates, which would entail undertaking a kind of psychology of the sacred, it is appropriate that we begin by describing how it appears to the simple consciousness and the qualities it assures for the one who experiences it. Next, we will examine the social mechanisms upon which the reality of the sacred is based and the social functions over which it presides.

Chapter II—THE AMBIGUITY OF THE SACRED

THERE IS SCARCELY ANY RELIGIOUS SYSTEM, EVEN IN THE broadest sense of the term, in which the categories of the pure and impure do not play a fundamental role. To the extent that the different aspects of collective behavior are differentiated and constitute relatively autonomous domains (politics, science, art, etc.), we see the words *pure* and *impure* acquiring new connotations, more precise than their traditional meaning, but by the same token, poorer.

PURITY AND INTERMIXTURE

The meanings of these terms are at present distinguished by an analysis that seems less a result of immaculate conception than of the very needs of civilization. They are merely connected by a loose interplay of relationships and metaphors. Moreover, it seems as if they had been indissolubly mixed at the outset and had served to express the many manifestations of a complex whole whose parts could not be isolated. The terms *pure* and *impure* have taken on all kinds of contradictions. Also, they continue to evoke a very special kind of quality, always present to some degree in the context in which they are used. In esthetics, we speak of the *purity* of a line, in chemistry, of a *pure* substance. It would seem that this original connotation is precisely what permits us to apply the same word to so different orders of reality. That is called pure, substance or line, whose essence is not mixed with anything that may alter or debase it. Pure is the wine unmixed with water, the precious metal without impurities, the man who has not known a woman, the healthy and living organism uncontaminated by the germs of death and destruction resulting from contact with a cadaver or blood.

THE PURE AND THE IMPURE: EQUIVOCAL FORCES

It must be admitted that the categories of pure and impure do not originally connote an ethical antagonism, but rather a religious polarity. They play the same role in the world of the sacred as the concepts of good and evil play in the world of the profane. For the world of the sacred, among other characteristics, is opposed to the world of the profane as a world of energy is opposed to a world of substance. On one side, forces, on the other side, things. The immediate result of this is of importance to the concepts of pure and impure. They become eminently mobile, interchangeable, and equivocal. In effect, if a *thing,* by definition, possesses a fixed nature, a *force,* on the contrary, implies good or evil according to the particular circumstances of its respective manifestations. It is good or bad not by nature but by the direction it takes or is given. We must not expect to see the qualities of the pure and impure affecting, in an invariant or exclusive way, any being, object, or status in which any religious effect is recognized. The one or the other is in turn attributed to them, to the extent that this effect takes place beneficently or malevolently, and simultaneously. This observation is enough to counterpoint Robertson Smith, who, in studying Semitic religions, affirms the original identity of the pure and the impure, against Marie-Joseph Lagrange, who insists upon their absolute independence. Every latent force simultaneously provokes desire and fear and stimulates in the believer the fear that it is the means of his undoing and the hope that it is the vehicle of his salvation. Each time that it is manifested, it is in a sense either a source of benediction or an avenue for malediction. In theory, it is equivocal, in actuality, it becomes univocal. From this point on, no hesitation is permitted. When impurity is encountered, which attacks the foundation of one's being, it is viewed as illness and symptom of death. The words that mean *purify* in "primitive" languages can be translated as *cure* or *disenchant*. Or again, purity is recognized as akin to health, to exuberant vitality, to excessive, irresistible force —dangerous because of its very intensity.

Sanctity and Defilement

It happens that defilement and sanctity, when duly identified, likewise entail caution and represent, as against the world of common usage, two poles of a dreadful domain. That is why they are designated by a unique term in the more advanced civilizations. The Greek word ἄγος, "defilement," also means, "the sacrifice which cleanses the defilement." The term ἅγιος, "holy," also means "defiled" according to an obsolete lexicographic usage. A distinction is made much later by recourse to two symmetrical words αγης, "pure," and εναγης, "accursed," the obvious construction of which indicates the ambiguity of the original word. The Greek ἀφοσιουν, the Latin *expiare*, "to expiate," are interpreted etymologically as "to rid (oneself) of the sacred (οσυος, *pius*) element that has been introduced by the defilement." Expiation is the act that permits the criminal to resume his normal activity and his place in the profane community, by ridding him of his sacred character, by *deconsecrating* himself, as de Maistre has earlier phrased it.

In Rome, it is well known that the word *sacer* designates, according to Ernout and Meillet's definition, "the one or that which cannot be touched without defilement." If someone becomes guilty of a crime against religion or the state, the assembled populace casts him out of its midst, in declaring him *sacer*. From this moment on, if there is any supernatural risk involved in putting him to death (*nefas est*), the murderer is at any rate regarded as innocent in terms of human law (*jus*) and is not condemned for homicide (*parricidii non damnantur*).

The more primitive civilizations do not separate linguistically the taboo caused by awe of sanctity from that inspired by fear of defilement. The same term evokes all the supernatural powers from which one ought to stay far removed, whatever the motive. The Polynesian *tapu* and Malay *pamali* designate approximately that which, blessed or accursed, is constrained in common usage, is not "free." In North America, the Dakota word *wakan* is used impartially for all kinds of miraculous or incomprehensible events. The natives not only apply it to missionaries and the Bible but also to the supreme impurity represented by females at times of menstruation. The ancient Japanese, in analogous fashion, used the term *kami* for both heavenly and earthly divinities and for "all malevolent and terrible creatures, objects of universal dread." Everything that possesses an efficacious property (*isao*) is *kami*.

THE SACRED DIALECTIC

It is in fact this quality (*mana*, if one prefers exotic terminology) that, in sum, stimulates the ambivalent feelings that have been described. One fears it and yet would like to avail oneself of it. It both repels and fascinates. It is taboo and dangerous. It suffices that one desires to approach and possess it at the very moment in which one is keeping a proper distance from it.

Thus is depicted, for example, the sacred character of the holy place (*hima*) in Semitic religions. There, it is forbidden to consummate the sexual act, to hunt game, to fell trees, or to cut grass. Legal jurisdiction ends at its boundary. The criminal who takes sanctuary there is immune to prosecution, consecrated as he is by the sanctity of the place. And for the same reason, any domestic animal that wanders in is lost to his owner. It is a place of utmost danger, one that cannot be entered with impunity. Yet, its temptations are forcefully described in an Arab proverb: "He who circles the *hima* will end by falling inside." One thinks of the butterfly, which cannot approach the flame without being hurt. Luther, speaking of the awe attached to holy places, states that it is mixed with fear. "And furthermore," he adds, "Far from fleeing, we draw nearer." Basically, the sacred stimulates in the believer exactly the same feelings as the fire does in the child—the same fear of being burnt, and the same desire to light it; the same anxiety in the face of the forbidden, the same faith that its conquest will afford him power and prestige, or injury and death in the event of failure. And just as the fire produces both evil and good, the sacred involves right or wrong action and is imbued with the opposing qualities of pure and impure, holy and sacrilegious, that define within their own limits the very frontiers to which the religious order can be extended.

One can thus, perhaps, grasp the essential mechanism involved in the sacred dialectic. Every force animating it tends to become dissociated. Its foremost ambiguity tends to resolve itself into antagonistic and complementary elements to which can be tendered, respectively, feelings of awe and aversion—feelings of desire and fervor that are inspired by its completely equivocal nature. But no sooner are these poles born of the extension of the sacred than they provoke, on their own part—to the precise degree that they possess sacred character—the same ambivalent reactions that had originally isolated them from each other.

The subdivision of the sacred produces good and evil spirits, priests and sorcerers, Ormazd and Ahriman, God and the devil. However, the attitudes of the believers toward each of these ramifications of the sacred reveal the very same ambivalence as their behavior with regard to the undivided manifestations of the sacred.

Confronted by the divine, Saint Augustine is chilled with horror and transported with love. *"Et inhorresco,"* he writes, *"et inardesco."* He explains that his horror comes about by his realization of the absolute disparity between his being and that of the sacred, and he explains his ardor by his awareness of their fundamental identity. Theology preserves this dual aspect of divinity, while distinguishing its terrifying and captivating sides, the *tremendum* and the *fascinans*, using once again R. Otto's terminology.

The *fascinans* corresponds to the intoxicating qualities

of the sacred, to the Dionysian giddiness, the ecstasy, the unity of transport. However, it is also, more simply, the bounty, the mercy, and the love of the divinity for what He has created that draws them irresistibly. On the other hand, the *tremendum* represents "divine wrath," the inexorable justice of the "jealous" God before whom the humbled sinner trembles and begs pardon. In the *Bhagavad-Gita,* Krishna appears before the hero Arjuna, who is terrified at seeing humans hurling themselves en masse into the God's mouth, like mountain streams flowing into the sea, "as the insect flies into the deadly flame." Some, with heads broken, remain suspended between his teeth, and the God's tongue thirsts for the entire generations that his throat has swallowed.

Analogously, the demonic, at the opposite pole of the sacred and sharing its terrible and dangerous characteristics, excites in its turn equally irrational sentiments that are opposed to one's self-interest. The devil, for example, is not only one who cruelly torments the damned in the inferno, but also one whose tempting voice offers the pleasure of earthly satisfactions to the anchorite. Without doubt, it is for his perdition, and the pact with the devil only assures transitory bliss, for it is clear that it could not be otherwise. It is no less remarkable that the tormentor appears simultaneously as the seducer and, if need be, as the comforter. Romantic literature, in exalting Satan and Lucifer, in endowing both with every charm, has merely portrayed their true nature, according to the very logic of the sacred.

Moreover, if the analysis of religion is oriented with reference to its extreme and opposing limits, representing in diverse forms salvation and damnation, its essential function seems simultaneously determined by a dual motive, the acquisition of purity and the elimination of defilement.

ACQUISITION AND LOSS OF PURITY

Purity is acquired by submitting to a set of ritualistic observances. The point above all (as Durkheim has well shown) is to become separated from the profane world in order to make possible the penetration of the sacred world without peril. The human must be abandoned before the divine can be reached. That is to say, rites of catharsis are to the highest degree negations or abstentions. They consist of temporary renunciations of the varied activities typical of the profane world, normal and necessary though they be to the preservation of life. In a certain sense, it is precisely to the degree that they seem normal or necessary that abstention is required. It is literally necessary to be purified in order to be worthy of approaching the domain of the Gods. It is always the intermixture that is feared. So, in order to savor divine life, all that is part of the ordinary process of human living must be rejected—speech, sleep, the company of others, nourishment, sexual relations. One who wishes to sacrifice, to enter the temple or to communicate with his God, must first interrupt his daily routine. He is enjoined to silence, vigils, retreats, inactivity, fasting, and continence. The restrictions that purify man and prepare him to confront the divine have the same value for the Australian neophyte who readies himself for the ordeal of initiation, for the magistrate of antiquity who offers a sacrifice in the name of the city, and for the modern Christian who kneels before the altar. Religious conceptions of the world always and everywhere require comparable renunciations of all who wish to approach the sacred. The more firm and dynamic these conceptions, the more demanding are the rules for purification. A genuine and voluntary transformation is required of the individual. In order to communicate with the divine, he must bathe, laying aside his ordinary clothing, and don clothes that are new, pure, or consecrated. He must shave his head, beard, and eyebrows and cut his nails (dead tissue, therefore bodily impurities). In extreme cases, he symbolically dies as a human and is reborn a God. For example, among the Vedas, the sacrificer while walking about the hearth closes his fists, covers his head, and imitates the movements of the foetus in the womb.

Thus consecrated and detached from the profane, he must stay removed from it so that his state of purity or consecration may last. Besides, this state cannot be maintained for very long. If life is to be preserved, he must recover the use of everything pertaining to it and incompatible with sanctity. On leaving the temple, the Ancient Hebrew priest takes off his sacred vestments "in order that his consecration should not spread," to quote Leviticus. The Vedic sacrificer plunges into a "ritual bath." He leaves in the water that which pertains to his religious nature and emerges once again profane, that is to say, free to use property and to participate in the collective life. One of the most valuable conclusions derived from the work of Hubert and Mauss on sacrifice pertains to these rites of entering and departing that facilitate passage from one world to the other, while respecting the autonomy of each.

PRECAUTIONS AGAINST DEFILEMENT AND SANCTITY

The use of property and participation in group life constitute and, in effect, define profane existence. The pure is excluded from it in order that the Gods may be approached, and the impure is banished lest its defilement be communicated to its surroundings. In fact, the community always takes extreme care to keep the latter isolated. They are easy to recognize, for in general, impure places are readily identified. Some are unique to the above mentioned societies, others are a result of wide diffusion. In the category of the impure can be placed the corpse, and by association, the parents of the deceased while in mourning, in other words, during the period that the virulence of the cadaver's defilement of them is greatest. The female at critical moments of her life, as when she appears bloody and wounded during her menses (and especially at her first menstruation) or in childbirth (particularly at the birth of her first child), is in the impure category until the purificatory ceremonial that reinstates her. The final sacrilege is that in which one, through bravado, imprudence, or accident, has violated a taboo, and especially the most serious of all taboos, that of incest.

These various impurities expose the entire community to danger, for nothing is more contagious than supernatural defilement. Thus, each society has as its first duty protection from defilement by rigidly excluding from its midst the bearers of germs. No relationships with the members of the group are allowed them, and the group tries to save itself from the ab-horrent poisons that the offenders contain and carry, elemen-tally and naturally. Young girls at puberty and women during menstrual periods are isolated in a special hut outside the vil-lage. They must not leave while in this state, or until a ritual purification has eliminated all vestiges of it. The oldest women in the village, immune because of their age and scarcely taking part in social life, prepare and bring them food. The vessels from which the recluses have eaten are broken and carefully buried. Their dwelling is so hermetically sealed that on occa-sion one of them may perish for lack of air. That is because of the need for preventing the sunlight from contracting their defilement while giving them light. Sometimes, for this reason, they are required to blacken their faces. Often, the building in which they are confined is constructed on a high platform so that the ground should not be contaminated. It is preferred that the patient be suspended in a hammock at the time of her indisposition. It is felt that this procedure effects almost abso-lute isolation.

It is remarkable that the same taboos that are a barrier to defilement also isolate one from contact with sanctity. The Emperor-God of the Mikado type, like the indisposed female, may not touch the ground or expose himself to the rays of the sun. This is not only true of the Japanese emperor but also of the Zapotec ruler and the heir to the throne, who lives for about sixteen years in a dark room. Equally, the dish from which the Mikado has eaten is broken, lest someone, who rashly uses it next, cause his mouth and throat to swell and be-come infected or cankerous. It is necessary at the same time to shelter the divine king from all defilement, from any dissipa-tion of his holy power, from any occasion for exerting it bru-tally. The proper functioning of nature and the state must be assured through diffusing this power slowly and carefully. By persistently turning his eyes in a given direction, the Mikado risks unleashing the worst calamities on the regions that he has "favored" unduly through potent emanations of his gaze.

Everything that is touched by a holy person is consecrated by this very act and can only be used by him. It suffices for him merely to name an object or bring his hand over it, and this removes it, to his profit, from the public domain. No one dares use it any more. Contact with it is fatal. The divine and the accursed, consecration and defilement, have exactly the same effects upon profane objects. They render them untouchable, withdraw them from circulation, and communicate to them their formidable qualities. So, one ought not be surprised that the same barriers are a protection against excesses of honor as of excesses of indignity, which would likewise deprive them, ordinarily, of the resources necessary to group survival and the powers indispensable for daily labor.

The Polarity of the Sacred

OPPOSITION OF THE TWO POLES OF THE SACRED

In addition, the pure and the impure must not be affected by characteristics contrary to their nature. The one attracts, the other repels. One is noble, the other ignoble. One provokes awe, love, and gratitude; the other distaste, horror, and terror. The pure, in the scholastic idiom of Lagrange, is defined as the *vitandum per accidens,* which man must avoid because of his very unworthiness when conditions are not appropriate for approaching it. The impure, on the contrary, corresponds to the *vitandum per se* because its very essence condemns one to isolation, and simple considerations of self-interest prompt one always to shun it. In the case of the pure, all positive powers are united and bound together, "those which preserve and lengthen life, which are conducive to health, social pre-eminence, bravery in war and excellence at work," according to R. Hertz's definition. These powers are exercised in harmony with nature, or rather comprise this harmony, and determine the rhythm of the universe. Thus, they seem marked by a "regulatory and august character that inspires veneration and confidence." At the other extreme are gathered the powers of death and destruction, the sources of illness, disorder, epidemics, and crimes, everything that enfeebles, diminishes, corrupts, and decays.

Everything in the universe is susceptible to dichotomization and can thus symbolize the varied, interrelated, and antagonistic manifestations of the pure and the impure. Living energies and the powers of death are joined to form the positive and negative poles of the religious world. To the former, belong the clearness and dryness of day; to the latter, the darkness and dampness of night. The East and the South seem to be the seat of the qualities of growth, which cause the sun to rise and become warmer. The West and the North are the habitat of the powers of perdition and ruin, which cause the star of life to descend and become extinguished. High and low become simultaneously distinguished—both the sky, which serves as the abode of the Gods in which death does not enter, and the subterranean world, which is reserved for the dark abode in which death's sway is absolute.

R. Hertz, who set up this dichotomy, made a profound study of it, in terms of *right* and *left*. We can see it applied to the least detail in ritual, in the practice of divination, in customs, and in beliefs. The Moslem steps with his right foot into a holy place and with his left foot into a place frequented by Djinns. A left-handed man is readily believed to be a sorcerer or possessed by a demon. One is reminded of the Christian saints who as infants refused the left breast of their mothers. The right hand is for the sceptre, for authority, for being sworn, and for good faith. The left is for fraud and treachery. Eve, through whom death is introduced into the world, is created out of one of Adam's left ribs. And it is the first woman, the prototype of a passive and disquieting breed, *l'enfant malade et douze fois impure,* who is regularly excluded from worship by various religions and regarded as sinner and sorceress. In representations of the Last Judgment, Jesus shows the sky to the elect with his right hand and the dreadful orifice of the inferno to the damned with his left hand. In depictions of the Crucifixion, the sun shines on the Lord's right, while the moon is drawn on His left, along with the bad thief and the synagogue.

Language itself manifests this opposition. In the Indo-European family, a special root expresses the concept of *right* in various languages. The *left* side, on the contrary, is designated by multiform and ambiguous terms, by devious expressions in which metaphor and antiphrasis play a large part. The same phenomenon has been observed by Meillet in the names of certain infirmities (deafness, lameness, and blindness[9] but to the *good right arm*[10] of the warrior, his *upright*-acteristic with the left. This quality of ill omen even necessitates the avoidance of calling them by their right names, and ever seeking new words that describe them only by indirection.

The word *droite* is also the word *adroite,* that which leads the *right* arm to its goal. Thus, attesting not only to the adroitness[9] but to the *good right arm*[10] of the warrior, his *uprightness,* it is proof that the Gods protect him. In China, the grand test of nobility is shooting with the longbow. It is not a test of competence or bravery, notes Granet, but "a musical ceremony, structured like a ballet." The arrow must be let fly on the proper note; the movements of the archers must *toucher au coeur;* the ritualized rules and a correct attitude of mind joined to the right attitude of body permit them to hit the center of the target. "Thus is virtue realized," concludes Li-K'uei.[11] The suzerains thus judge the uprightness of their vassals by their ability to aim their arrows well. In Greek, the word αμαρτάνω, which means to commit an error, a mistake, or even a sin, originally meant "to miss the target." We now understand the different meanings of the word "right," designated manual dexterity, the rightness of an argument, a legal norm, rectitude of character, purity of intentions, the basic goodness of an act—in a word, everything that, physically or metaphysically, directs the *right* power to its goal. Conversely, *gaucherie* is a sign of evil intent and an augury of failure. It is at once maladroitness, at once cause and effect of every tortuous, crooked, or oblique power, of every false calculation or maneuver. It is everything uncertain and everything that falls short of its goal; and that which is uncertain and cause of suspicion and fear, all that is imperfect, exposes and involves a tendency toward wrong-doing. Right and adroit manifest purity and divine favor, left and maladroit exemplify defilement and sin.

THE REVERSIBILITY OF PURE AND IMPURE

Regarded as similar from a certain point of view by the profane world to which they are equally opposed, each in its own sphere extremely hostile to the other, the pure and the impure share power that it is permissible to utilize. The more intense the force, the more promising its efficaciousness. From this derives the temptation to change defilement into benediction, to make the impure an instrument of purification. For this purpose, recourse is had to the mediation of the priest, the man whose sanctity renders him capable of approach without fear of impurity. In all cases, he knows the rites that preserve him from suffering it. He possesses the power and knows the means of turning the malign power of infection toward good, of transforming a threat of death into an assurance of life.

When mourning is ended, purificatory ceremonies not only free the parents of the deceased from his defilement, they also mark the moment at which the dead person, bearer of evil and fearful power, and all the characteristics of the left-sided sacred, becomes a tutelary spirit, beseeched with awe and reverence. Analogously, the remains of the cadaver become relics. Horror is changed to trust.

A female in childbirth must be isolated from the group in order to keep it from contamination. But at the same time, among the Herero for example, each morning the milk of all the cows of the village is brought to her so that contact with her mouth should assure its purity. Among the Warrundi, a girl at her first menses is guided around the house by her grandfather, who makes her touch everything, so that everything should be sanctified by her.

In the same way, the Romans sprinkled the garden of Anna Perenna with *virgineus cruor* as this menstrual blood commonly serves to destroy garden parasites. Moreover, menstrual blood from childbirth is used as a remedy for other impurities—boils, itching, skin diseases, and leprosy. The more impure it is, the more potent it is considered. Thus, the blood from a young girl's first menstruation or from a woman's first childbirth is preferred. Yet, what deadly power is not attributed to this terrifying flow? There is no abomination of which Pliny the Elder does not accuse it. "It would be difficult to find anything more monstrous in its effects than this periodic flow. It turns new wine sour, renders grain unproductive, kills young shoots and desiccates garden produce. Fruit falls from the trees under which a woman in this state has sat. Her reflection alone tarnishes shining mirrors, dullens the sword's edge, erases the lustre of ivory. Multitudes die, even brass and iron rust, and acquire a detestable odor. Dogs that have tasted it become rabid, and venom from their bite is incurable, etc."

Even today the idea is more or less consciously dominant that the more repugnant and dangerous the remedy, the more efficacious it is. Also, one systematically seeks ingredients in compounding panaceas that are the most repulsive, physically, and the most impure, religiously. The Arabs use against Djinns and the evil eye a mixture made out of excrement, menstrual blood, and bones of the dead. To be comprehensive, they finish the medicine by adding to it some of the remains of the sacrificial victim. This scapegoat, charged by the Semites with the sins of all the people, is viewed as the quintessence of defilement. The altar is annointed with its blood. The lustral water that is used to purify the tent and furniture of the deceased and of those who have touched the corpse must contain the ashes of the heifer offered up for the sin. The priest who has cremated the victim outside the camp and the *pure man* who gathered up its ashes must wash their bodies and clothing. They are impure until evening, as are all those who have touched the purificatory water, or who themselves are to be purified with it. The entire book of Leviticus can be interpreted from this point of view. Each verse proves the intimate connection between the pure and the impure.

In Greece, remarks Gernet, "Whatever is a source of impurity or cause of taboo can be an obligatory object for consecration." In fact, Athenian maidens offered to Artemis the first napkin stained with their menstrual blood, and the clothing of dead women and women who had given birth were consecrated to Artemis-Iphigenia of Brauron.

Not only objects but beings harbor the ambiguous power of the sacred. The protective spirits painted on the hat of the Siberian shaman are colored half red and half black, in order to show the two ways in which their power is exercised. Among the Lapps, those killing a bear are covered with glory, however, they are at first regarded as impure and assigned a special dwelling. They remove the clothing worn when killing the beast. They bring its meat to their wives, while feigning to be strangers. Their seclusion ends only after a purificatory turn about a fire. Similarly, in South Africa, to kill a formidable beast—lion, leopard or rhinoceros—is considered a brilliant feat, but before an honor guard can, with great pomp, escort the lucky hunter into the village, he must atone for his great deed in a distant hut, where his body is painted white and he is fed by uncircumcised boys. The same warrior having slain an enemy in a raid, if he is to be honored, is not reintegrated into the community before being cleansed of the blood that he has spilled, of the contamination contracted through murder and touching a corpse.

Conversely, the impurity acquires a mysterious power, or, what amounts to the same thing, manifests or is proof of it for the person heroically exposed to the perils of sacrilege. When Oedipus, accused of the grave abominations of parricide and incest, steps on Athenian soil, he seems to be sacred and proclaims himself a source of benediction for his country. Among the Ba-Ila, nothing is more monstrous or dreadful than incest, yet one wishing to succeed in his enterprise commits incest with his sister, for "this imbues his talisman with great power." The Thongan who wants to hunt a hippopotamus has sexual intercourse with his daughter. Thus he becomes a "murderer," but he now has the power to accomplish "great things on the river." There is a tribe in the vicinity of Lake Nyassa where incest with a mother or sister makes the person daring it immune to bullets. By violating the most sacred of taboos, man acquires the perilous co-operation of supernatural forces, almost like signing a pact with the devil in order to become a sorcerer. Through incest, the daring one is immediately transformed into a sorcerer, but only for a limited time, for the accomplishment of a particular deed. He must ritually brave the hazards of sacrilege in order to place himself beyond the reach of profane dangers.

It is literally sufficient for a conversion obtained through appropriate penance, for a change of meaning facilitated by appropriate practices or attitudes, for the sinister power of which the transgressor of the sacred rules has given proof, that it remain intact and in its opposing form when it is a question of maintaining and respecting these rules. Thus the high priest P. Licinius, says Titus Livius, stopped Caius Flaccus from becoming a priest of Jupiter "because of his turbulent and debauched youth." And the latter, previously detested by his parents for his vices, was so transformed by his subsequent consecration that he restored the sanctity of his priesthood, which had been compromised by his predecessors. In the same way, if in Christian hagiography the greatest sinners make the greatest saints, it is not merely in order to edify the faithful with the omnipotence of divine grace, but also by its illustration, always possible in the sacred order, of the exceptional powers manifested by the enormity of their sins.

THE ELIMINATION OF INEXPIABLE DEFILEMENT

It so happens that crime discourages reparation. Society finds itself stunned and frightened in the face of too great blemishes upon the sacred. Its priests despair of changing or effacing them. The defilement that has been suffered seems inexpiable, that is to say, restoring to the word its etymological meaning, that no purificatory rite can rid the offender of the powerful element with which he was imbued when he committed the forbidden act. There is no longer any means of "liberating" him, of enabling him to re-enter the profane order. Therefore, the only thing left is to extirpate radically this principle and this base of dangerous contagion. Thus, it is declared *sacred* (*sacer*, ιεροϲ). The group does not readily agree to put him to death for execution presumes contact, and there is a risk of the defilement that they desire to remove passing on to them. As a result, the criminal is exiled, conducted without arms or provisions to the frontier of the nation's territory. The task of destroying him is left to foreigners, beasts, or the elements. If the guilty one is an animal—for example, a goat that has eaten its excrement, an ox that has struck the ground with its tail, or a dog that has mated with a pig—and his owner cannot afford to lose the animal, it is sold to itinerant traders, and the evil let fall upon them.

The offender is frequently delivered to the mercies of the sea in a boat without sails. Sometimes, for greater security, his hands are tied and the skiff is scuttled. According to old Norwegian law, the outlaw is left in a boat that leaks from every part. When the state takes charge of making the plague-bearer disappear, or in effect delegates a man or office for this function, they too become subject to the same opprobrium and must remain apart from the community, as if they had assumed the total burden of the defilement from which they deliver the community. The magistrates who are responsible take the strictest precautions lest, at the time of execution, the fearful contagion spread to the group.

The impure vestal virgin is buried alive; to shed her blood would contaminate the city. She and her defilement are made to disappear into the bowels of the earth. In fact, this is a very serious matter. It is a question of a sacred being. The sanctity of the offender increases the weight of the sin, just as the gravity of past sins is sometimes a criterion of future sanctity. The priestess is carried to her punishment in a hermetically sealed litter. It is important that any communication with the citizenry be impossible. The very sound of the impure one's voice must not reach their ears, for in the case of such a sacrilege, anything can serve as a means of defilement. The condemned leaves the litter veiled and immediately climbs down into the trench, which has already been dug and which is sealed without delay. She is left a negligible quantity of food. Antigone, whom Creon led to her tomb by a *deserted*

path, accepted readily enough in order "to avoid sacrilege and
protect the entire community from defilement."

Her very impurity renders the criminal sacred. It has become dangerous to make an attempt on her life directly. In
leaving some food for the entombed vestal virgin, the city
acquits itself of responsibility and leaves it for the Gods to
assume. (As G. Glotz has well shown, this is the principle back
of the ordeal.) The offender has entered the world of the divine. Her salvation or doom is now up to the Gods. Men
deliver her to them, and for this reason let her leave the community *alive*.

It is no less important to protect nature than society from
virulence and impurity. Nothing is more significant in this
regard than the punishment of the *culeus,* reserved by the
Romans for parricide and sacrilege. Complete isolation of the
offender is sought. Wooden shoes are put on him, his head is
covered with the skin of a wolf, and before throwing him into
the sea, he is enclosed in a leather sack together with a serpent,
a cock, and a dog, to which the defilement can be harmlessly
transferred. It is the translation of the ancient curse against
one whose transgression seems irreparable: "Let neither land
nor sea receive his bones." The wolf skin, the wooden shoes,
and the sewed-up leather sack represent many precautions for
preventing the witch's impurity from contaminating the earth,
air, and water of the sea, as Cicero notes in discussing punishment, a condition capable of purifying all other defilements.

Cohesion and Dissolution

SOCIAL DISTRIBUTION OF THE PURE AND THE IMPURE

We can now map a kind of social geography of the pure
and the impure. It is a neutral zone that they contest and to
which they are banished for identical reasons and with contradictory attitudes of mind. There, every force appears in
turn pure or impure, susceptible to being directed either way
without the possibility of permanently attributing such ambiguity to it. The powers of evil and good are equally stimu-

lated; ill luck and good luck are equally attracted. Thus, we see that sexual intercourse favors the reaping of the harvest, just as, among the Bantu, the inflammation of a wound or the quality of an illness activates the purifying quality of lustral water. But this very ambiguity presupposes a more stable distribution, a polarity better guaranteeing good or evil. Each of these opposing principles seems in effect to enjoy a fixed habitat. On the one side, the majestic and ordered world of the king, the priest, and the law from which one must fearfully keep one's distance; on the other side, the sinister domain of the pariah, the sorcerer, and the criminal from which one must, in horror, stay away. Those who, by nature, purify, cure, pardon, and protect through their sanctity are opposed to those who, in essence, defile, debase, and mislead—being dealers in sin and death. The clothes of the prince, splendid and dazzling with gold and flawless diamonds, are merely the luminous counterpart of the vile decay and melted flesh of the state of decomposition.

Indeed, the sovereign and the cadaver, like the warrior and the menstruating woman, incarnate to the highest degree the hostile forces of the pure and impure. Death brings defilement, and the prince rids one of it. No contact is permitted between them. Beings imbued with sanctity, like Polynesian chiefs, objects that seem to be teeming reservoirs of sanctity, like Australian *churingas,* are isolated by the strictest taboos from any possible source of infection, such as dead tissue or menstrual blood.

In this regard, certain sacred rules limiting the liberty of the high priest must be recalled. He is not only forbidden to touch a corpse but even to approach the funeral pyre, to hear the sound of funeral flutes, and to pronounce the names of vegetables or animals that play a part in the cult of the dead. His boots must not be made from the skins of animals that have died a natural death. In the same way, the Kaffir high priest must not visit cemeteries or walk along paths leading to the fields in which corpses are putrifying. Entry into the room of the deceased is forbidden to him until an effigy of the deceased has been constructed, thus proving that he has

become a beneficent and venerable force. In the tragedy of
Euripedes, Artemis leaves Hippolytus dying, for a Goddess is
not permitted to look upon a cadaver, and the last breaths of
the dying must not defile a pure gaze. At the time of the festival of the Anthesteria in Athens, when the souls of the dead
return from the underworld and wander the streets of the
city, the temples are surrounded with ropes to prevent them
from approaching.

LOCALIZATION OF THE PURE AND IMPURE

So rigid a separation of the pure and impure principles
implies their distinct localization at the social center. In fact,
the center would seem to be the clear and comforting abode of
the pure, and the periphery the dark and disquieting abode
of the impure. The sacred powers reside in the brilliantly
colored totem poles, the pride of the village square where the
altar and the men's lodge or the special hut of the chief are
jointly erected. In New Caledonia, this hut is called *moaro,*
and *moaro* is also the name of the clan. The altar is designated
by the term *kamoaro,* "that which is the *moaro.*" There is no
better way of emphasizing the identification of the entire collectivity with the altar and the big hut, which are the foci for
the ordering of its existence. For the Kanakas, there is a
similar reality, Leenhardt writes, whose earthly embodiment
is the great hut, whose social reflection is the clan, and whose
projection toward the invisible is the altar. The forces that
animate the life of the village and exalt its glory are thus sup-
ported by its center, and in passing through the square, imbue
it with beneficial strength. They move centrifugally, radiating
out of idyllic space replete with sanctity in which the Gods
dwell, toward which ascends the smoke of sacrificial fires, from
which eventually come the ruler's edicts. Little by little, their
influence is replaced by that of the malevolent and mysterious
presences of the brush, whose converging pressure is in danger
of engulfing everything. Anyone passing by unconsciously en-
croaches upon their domain to the degree that he moves away
from the center, and before becoming completely exposed to

their sinister power, he has already passed the dreaded hut in which are confined menstruating women, women in childbirth, or warriors returned from battle, all waiting to be purified from the blood that they have spilt—in short, all the defiled, who must be isolated from the radiant and animating center of collective life.

These locations are far from coincidental. They are encountered at all levels of civilization. R. Hertz has rightly observed that the dichotomy of right and left is analogous to that of inside and outside. The community views itself as enclosed, as in an imaginary pregnancy. Inside the circle, all is light, legality, and harmony; space is marked-off, ruled, and distributed. At the center, the ark of the covenant or the altar represents the material and active base for the sanctity that diffuses outward to the circumference. From there, extends the outer darkness, the world of ambushes and traps, which knows neither authority nor law, and from which emanates a constant dread of defilement, illness, and damnation. In circling the sacred fire, the believers so place themselves as to turn their right shoulders toward the center from which good luck originates, and their left sides, the defensive and inferior parts of their bodies (left arms carrying shields), are turned toward the somber, hostile, and anarchic outside. This circling encloses the beneficent powers on the inside. At the same time it forms a barrier against dreaded attacks from the outside.

The layout of modern cities even makes understandable, through a fixed plan, the part mythical and part objective value of such an arrangement. At the center, the church or cathedral (seat of the divine), the town hall, government buildings, courts (symbols and temples of power and authority), theaters, museums, monuments to the dead, statues of great men (various aspects of the city's sacred heritage) benefit from large squares, broad avenues, and gardens in bloom. At night, dazzling lights afford splendor and security to these privileged quarters. Around this protective nucleus, warm and official, is built up a zone of shadow and misery—the streets of which are narrow, ill-lighted, and unsafe, in which are located decrepit hotels, hovels, and various clandestine establishments in which are probably gathered prowlers, prostitutes, and criminals of every description. Where cemeteries have not already been swallowed up by the city's expansion, they are located here, and at nightfall, it is hard to pass by without feeling a slight chill. Thus, the opposition of pure and impure, in passing from the religious to the secular domain and becoming an opposition of law and crime, of life of honor against dissolute existence, has retained the ancient topography of supernatural principles—good at the center and evil at the periphery.

COHESION AND DISSOLUTION

In a general way, the sacred powers inhabit a fixed locale. The empire of defilement, on the contrary, is diffused and indeterminate. We have been able to see, especially in Australia, a fundamental opposition between religion and magic. In fact, the evil spirits from which Australian sorcerers derive their power are not bound to any special totemic center. Like the magicians themselves, they exist outside the social group. The impure force that they exert, according to Strehlow's definition, that "which suddenly ends life or leads to the death of anyone coming in contact with it," does not belong to a recognized clan, is not in a public place, does not direct the formation of any system of morals, as the church or the established religion directs the body politic. On the contrary, it does not take into account local peculiarities. Indeed it favors those (women or slaves) who are excluded from the regular cults.

One can say that it is the very emanation of the brush, formidable and continually an enemy, engulfing in its homogeneity as the sea inundates islets and the various human groups that have successfully established their habitations upon it. It is in the brush, far from the village, that the sorcerer is initiated. He comes back with a personal tutelary spirit that is in opposition to the clan, worshipping its collective totem. The clan allows members of other groups to consume the totemic animal to which it is bound. Indeed, the economic organization of the tribe seems to be based on reciprocal dietary taboos. But the magician to whom an animal is revealed as allied in the course of a dream, hallucination, or trance, or to whom a related sorcerer has bequeathed the title of protective spirit, is protected and revered by the other members of the community. He is viewed by the clan as a foreign element, besides wielding a mysterious and dreaded power. He is no longer regarded by others as a "brother." In fact, he has become another being. The spirits that have initiated him have changed his vital organs and have injected into his body pieces of rock crystal in which reside the powers that cause him to be feared. People flee from him, and he leads a solitary and hunted existence. He becomes virtually outcast from the community, and in contrast to the cohesion of the community, he incarnates, through the principles of death, the very forces of dissolution.

The words *cohesion* and *dissolution* permit us to define adequately the respective unity of the complex wholes to which the pure and impure belong. The powers defining the former are those that affirm, solidify, and strengthen, that make one vigorous, sound, stable, and predictable. In the universe, they preside over cosmic harmony. In society, they make for material prosperity and good administration. In man, they buttress the integrity of his physical being. They are everything that founds, maintains, or perfects norms, order, and health. It is understood that they are incarnate in the ruler. The powers defining the latter are responsible for dissipation, disorder, and fever. To them is imputed every irregularity in the normal course of events. They are the cause of eclipses, marvels, monsters, the birth of twins, and in general, manifestations of ill omen that result from their encounter with natural laws and that necessitate expiation—such as trees blooming in wintertime, darkness occurring at high noon, protracted pregnancies, and epidemics.

To them are equally attributed transgressions against the political or religious order. In fact, we have observed that treason, sacrilege, and regicide are regarded as inexpiably impure.

That is because they strike at social cohesion, place it in jeopardy, and tend to destroy it. Sometimes, not conforming to the opinion of others is sufficient grounds for exclusion from the society. In China, the councilor who does not share the opinions of his colleagues compromises the destiny of the kingdom, for all decisions must be made unanimously. He is then forced to resign his office and go into exile. In yielding, the one who has taken the responsibility for protest only "engenders hate."[12] In going off, he would restore the cohesion that his continued presence would threaten. The exile cuts all his ties to country and family. He cannot take the vessel of his patrimonial cult with him. The text of the Li-K'uei, with commentaries by Marcel Granet, that prescribes the conduct of the emigrating adversary, must be read:

> As soon as he has crossed the frontier, he levels a plot of ground and makes a mound. He turns his face toward his country and makes loud lament. He is clad in a tunic, an undergarment, a white hat without ornamentation and without colored edging [*attitude of mourning*]. He wears shoes of untanned leather, the axle of his carriage is covered with the skin of a white dog, his team of horses have not had their hair trimmed. He himself stops cutting his nails, beard, and hair. When he takes his meals, he abstains from pouring any libation [*he is cut off from communion with the Gods*]. He abstains from denying his guilt [*he also abstains from admitting his guilt; only a chief has enough courage and authority to admit formal guilt*]. His wives (or at least his first wife) are not allowed near him [his sex life and his domestic relations are interrupted]. Only at the end of three months may he again don his ordinary clothing.

When he emerges from the period of mourning, the protesting vassal no longer has a country. He is a man from nowhere who has no place in any kingdom. Such is the terrible fate reserved for the man who behaves individualistically in the community to which he belongs and to which his attitude and contagious example is a catalytic agent of dissolution.

On the family level, the problem is no different. Infractions that threaten to destroy familial organization are equally regarded as sacrilegious, hence, the extreme severity of the measures that render harmless the incestuous person and the parricide, declared by the Romans to be *sacer*. Finally, to complete this classification of defilements that cause dissolution, illness, which attacks man's physical powers, must be added. The blood lost by women who are menstruating or giving birth is feared, and most dreaded is the *decomposition* of a cadaver, the most impressive image of ultimate and inevitable dissolution, of the triumph of the destructive forces that also dangerously undermine biological survival and the well-being of the universe and the society. The corpse itself is a *wanderer*, a *soul in pain,* so much so that burial and funeral rites have not enabled the one whose transgression has cut him off from the living to enter the company of the dead. He only becomes a beneficent force once he has been reintegrated.

PURITY AND IMPURITY: "AUTONOMOUS STATES"

It seems that the concepts of pure and impure originally had not been separated from the many sentiments that in their different manifestations stimulate the complementary and antithetical forces, whose *concordia discors* structures the universe. Their opposition has more recently been limited by hygienic or moral considerations. A state can be comprehended in which this opposition is indissolubly mixed with other antagonisms that are so intermingled and interpenetrated as to make it impossible to order or distinguish them. Purity is, therefore, simultaneously health, vigor, bravery, luck, longevity, dexterity, wealth, good fortune, and sanctity. Impurity comprises illness, weakness, cowardice, gaucherie, infirmity, bad luck, misery, misfortune, and damnation. It is no longer possible to perceive moral aspirations. Physical defect and frustration are equally blamed with perverse desires and regarded as symptoms or results. Reciprocally, adroitness or success manifest divine favor and seem to be an assurance of virtue.

Ancient civilizations permit us to follow the continuous moral conceptualization of these ideas step by step. They re-

ceived them as supernatural ideas but passed them on to pos-
terity in ethical or secular form. In Babylon, we observe that
states of grace or of sin are still described as autonomous.[13]
The criminal is the prey of demoniacal powers:

> "Malediction rises from the sea, grace descends from the skies.
> . . . Where (falls) the wrath of the Gods, [demons] rush about
> shrieking. They grasp the man whose God has abandoned him
> and envelop him like a robe. They come right at him, fill him
> with poison, tie his hands and bind his feet. They press upon
> his flanks, and pour their venom into him."

Like decay, complete restoration is his concern:

> "May the malediction, charm, pain, suffering, illness, misery,
> sin and sickness, which is in my body, flesh and limbs, be
> peeled like this onion. Now, may the burning Girru consume
> it, may the spell disappear, and may I see the light."

EVOLUTION OF THE CONCEPTS OF THE PURE AND IMPURE

Shortly thereafter, Greek thought distinguished between
these heterogeneous notions, the more elementary analysis regarded as an indivisible unity. By painstaking analysis, each
concept is elaborated and assigned a definite place in the hierarchy of accidents and functions, of deeds or intentions, with
which man's existence and mind are concerned. It is above all,
thanks to the mysterious morality enclosed in the Orphic circles, thanks to the Pythagorean table of contraries, and thanks
to the Manichaean cosmology that various concepts can be
defined and made precise. Taxonomy and philosophic reflection analyze their qualities. Without doubt they always correspond, their basic affinity is perceived, but they themselves
are finally isolated, each subsumed under the rubric defining
its essence. The opposition between left and right now belongs
to geometry, that of even and odd to arithmetic, that of clean
and dirty to hygiene, that of health and disease to medicine.
In addition, the dichotomy of good and evil is reserved for
ethics, and religion retains the opposition of grace and sin.
More and more, purity, properly speaking, is identified with

physical or moral cleanliness, and essentially with chastity. Purity represents the point of departure from which the idea of defilement may in some way be removed. From the miasma that the current carries off, it has become the stain of which the soul is purified by divine forgiveness.

PROFANE AND SACRED

Through all religious history, the notion of the sacred has retained a very special uniqueness that confers upon it an incontestable unity, however variable seem the civilizations in which it is observed, from the crudest to the most complex, however reduced its influence may be in modern times. It continues opposing "the way, the truth, and life" to the powers that corrupt existence in every sense of the word, that make it despair and consign it to damnation. However, at the same time it displays, in whatever supports it, the essential connivance of the exalting and the ruinous. The profane is the world of ease and security. It is bounded by two abysses. Two stumbling blocks attract man when ease and security no longer satisfy him, when he is weighed down through safe and prudent submission to rules. He then understands that the latter is only there as a barrier, that this is not what is sacred, but rather what is unattainable, and will only be known and understood by one who has passed or broken it. The barrier once surmounted, no return is possible. One must walk continuously on the road to sanctity or the road to damnation, which abruptly join at unforseen crossroads. He who dares to set the subterranean powers in motion is one who is not content with his lot, or sometimes one who has been unable to sway the heavens. He is determined to force entry. The pact with the devil is no less consecrating than divine grace. The one who has signed it and the one burdened by it are equally separated forever from the common lot and, by the prestige of their destiny, trouble the dreams of the timid and the jaded, who have not attempted to plumb the depths.

Chapter III—THE SACRED AS RESPECT:

THEORY OF TABOO

THE TWO POLES OF THE SACRED ARE GENERALLY OPPOSED to the profane world. When faced with it, their antagonism shrinks and tends to disappear. Sanctity fears alike both defilement and the profane, which represent different degrees of impurity. Inversely, defilement is no less capable of contaminating sanctity than the profane, which can equally be attacked. Thus, the three elements of the religious universe—the pure, the profane, and the impure—manifest a remarkable aptitude for any two to ally themselves against the third. We have seen how this dialectic operated within the sacred sphere, how each of the two terms, in opposing the other, automatically confronted the sacred with the kind of *néant actif* that constitutes the profane.

The basic ambiguity of the sacred being admitted, it must now-be noted how it is altogether opposed to the world of the profane. That is to say, we must investigate what in society corresponds to the distinction between the two complementary and antithetical domains of the sacred and the profane. We soon perceive that it overlaps or embraces other divisions or dichotomies—that of equally complementary and antithetical groups or principles whose opposition and agreement (the *concordia discors*) enable the group to function. So signifies, for example, the pairing of moieties in societies in which power is diffused, or the pairing of ruler and subjects in societies where power is concentrated. In these two extreme yet abstract types (in reality, they never are present in their pure state), the division into two "parts"—equal in weight and prestige, or balanced in unequal and inverse weight and prestige (one compensating for the other)—delineates the conception of the order of the universe. At the same time and in the same way, this division governs the allocation of the profane and the sacred. What is free for the members of one moiety is forbidden to the members of the other. What is permitted to the ruler is forbidden to his subjects, and vice versa. The function of taboos is to protect the established order from all sacrilegious attack. They cannot be considered separately. They form a system from which no element can be removed and which can only be explained by a total functional analysis of the society in which they are enforced.[14]

The Structure of the Universe

BIFURCATION OF SOCIETY

Among the important facts clarified by the study of totemistic societies, it is permissible to consider the majority in terms of the division into moieties in tribal organization. Moieties, in fact, represent much more than an intermediary between tribe and clans. They represent nothing less than the basic and constant framework of social unity. Clans vary in number, seeming to increase or decrease. The number of moieties on the contrary is assumed to be fixed. A tribe comprises two, and only two, of them. The rare cases in which a tripartite division has been verified can easily be subsumed under the general rule. Thus, among the Masai of East Africa, one observer distinguishes three main groups, but another observer regards as primary a clan described by the first as a subdivision. He describes the population as divided into four basic groups, which are paired on expeditions. The members of the first pair bear in common the name, *red blooded beasts.* The others are called *black beasts.*

Also, clan lines are sometimes flexible and vague. The rules of clan exogamy are often weakened, while they are enforced between moieties. Finally, clans frequently seem like the segmentation of a bipartite frontal division. Hence, the presence of moieties can basically be viewed as a special phenomenon of totemistic societies in the very wide generality of their geographic occurrence.

It is important to verify with concrete cases the nature and principle characteristics of this bipartite division upon which depends the system of taboos that, for each of the two moieties of the society, divides the world into profane and sacred domains. In Australia, members of the moieties are most of the time scattered in various places, but in each of them this opposition persists, and when the tribe is gathered together, regrouping into moieties is once again of prime importance. From the beginning, it is established that the system of moieties prevails over all others in tribal organization. Durkheim and Mauss have shown that all nature was apportioned according to the social divisions of the tribe. Their work, a study of subdivision into clans, which actually constitute the most sharply differentiated groups in Australian society, is especially valuable for regrouping them into moieties, if it is true, as the authors are convinced, that clans are derived from the moieties through binary fission. Indeed, if it is difficult to account for the choice of clan totems and their respective properties, the names of the moieties' totems seem, by contrast, obviously much clearer. The creatures that are the totemic symbols are in fact of different colors and often antagonistic to each other. The Gournditch-Mara of the state of Victoria are divided into *krokitch* (white cockatoos) and *kaputch* (black cockatoos). These same designations are found in various other tribes. Sometimes, as in Mount Gambier, mere clans have white or black cockatoos for a totem. But each of these belongs to a moiety, and the latter has a name clearly related to the terms *Krokitch* and *Kaputch* of the Gournditch-Mara. It is tempting, therefore, to see in these cockatoo clans the basic tribal division, namely the moieties themselves.

Hence, in these tribes the totems of the moieties are not haphazard. They are symmetrical and antithetical. They are animals of the same species, but of contrasting colors. They appear in this way to be identical and antagonistic at the same time. The white and black cockatoos are opposed, just as are the red blooded and the black beasts among the Masai.

BIFURCATION OF THE UNIVERSE

This symmetry and opposition are preserved in the division of the elements of the universe between the social structures. The work of Durkheim and Mauss demonstrates that beings or objects are classed in the same division because of the mutual affinities that they manifest. For example, the grass upon which the clan's totemic animal feeds, and the animals that are habitually encountered in the clan's habitat, are placed in the same class. Among the Aranda, frogs are associated with the eucalyptus because they are found in its hollow. The parrot is allied to the kangaroo, because it is ordinarily observed flying in its vicinity. Conversely, it seems certain that objects that are opposed, and paired in their opposition, are distributed among groups that are socially opposed and paired. That is, for example, the case generally with the moon and the sun. In the Mackay area, the sun is *yungaroo*, the moon *wootaroo*. In the Mount Gambier tribe, not only is a star assigned to each moiety, but inside the moieties, in antithetical clans, are classed white and black cockatoos.

It is true that occasionally the opposition is not so sharp. The moieties' totems among many Australian tribes, notably in New South Wales, are in fact the eagle-hawk and the crow. But these are always at least similar creatures, two birds represented in myths as perpetually at war with each other. In tribal games, equally, each moiety is opposed to the other, in its entirety. If one passes from the least distinct to the most clear cut cases, one begins to perceive better the systematic nature of the moieties' antagonism. The Aranda are divided into *land* and *water* clans. The same terms are used at Mabuiag, an island in the Torres Straits, where in addition, the totems of one of the moieties are aquatic animals and those of the other, terrestrial or amphibious animals. In these latter cases, the moieties are opposed like two contrary elements, and this opposition extends to all manifestations of collective life. One resides in the east, the other in the west; one camps leeward, the other windward, etc.

This aspect seems even more marked in the other large totemic area, North America. The Zuni actually reflect a relatively complex ecological organization. The clans that have been observed also seem to be derived from two original moieties. In any case, their mythology suggests it. When the world began, a magician presented two pairs of eggs of contrasting colors to mankind—one pair dark blue as the *sky,* the other dark red as the *earth.* In one he specified, *winter* exists, and in the other, *summer.* He invited man to make a choice. The first ones selected the blue eggs. The birds escaping from them had black feathers. These were the *crows,* which flew *north* (the north is the winter season). The others selected the red eggs, from which *parrots* emerged. Their properties were those of seeds, warmth and peace. (These are the attributes of the *south* and of summer, just as destruction and war are those of winter.) That is why, concludes the informant, the Zuni were divided into winter and summer clans, or into crows and parrots.

This system, vestiges of which have survived among the Pueblo Indians, opposes colors, seasons, and the principles of war and peace—that is to say, socially determined phenomena —through the medium of birds of different species. This last distinction is the basis for the conflict between moieties of various Siouan tribes (the Osage of Missouri, the Creek of Alabama, etc.). One is devoted to deeds of war, the other to works of peace. In camp, one is located to the right, the other to the left of the entrance-way. Analogous divisions are not rare. The moieties are located in one or the other half of the camp circle. In time, as among the Ponka, the clans contained within the moieties correspond to opposing elements or principles on a face-to-face basis. For example, the water clan is situated facing the fire clan, the wind clan facing the earth clan. Shortly, these principles or elements are represented by a clan in each moiety, as among the Omaha. Clans with the same symbol then are lodged facing each other on each side of the thoroughfare of the encampment, each contained in its respective moiety, for example, the two thunder clans facing each other at the camp entrance.

The constant function of these North American moieties is to produce ritual tournaments for the group and periodic games of an athletic character. Such is the case among the Iroquois, whose moieties compete at Lacrosse, or among the Winnebago of Wisconsin, who play ball. The ceremonies for which the entire tribe gathers are occasions reserved for contests between moieties. These are directed by a spokesman, and each performs the dances appropriate to its character, while the other witnesses the spectacle.

In fact, their very names indicate that they partition the universe, and this division applies to social institutions as well as to nature. Thus, among the Hupa of northern California, one of the moieties has exclusive possession of eel medicine, the other of salmon medicine. The exogamous moieties of the Winnebago—one divided into four the other into eight clans, also exogamous by derivation—are symbolically connected with the sky and the earth. Their members are designated as "above" and "below," confronting each other on most social occasions. Each clan performs the rites properly belonging to it and assumes particular political functions. The bear clan is occupied with public policy; the chief of the tribe is from the thunderbird clan; the public hawker from the Bison clan. The Miwok are equally divided into two exogamous patrilineal moieties, the water or bull-frog moieties, and earth or blue-jay. Now all natural phenomena are related to earth and water—with implications for one or the other moiety, following their manifest affinities somewhat arbitrarily, and symbolic correspondences playing the greatest role.[15]

COMPLEMENTARY QUALITIES

An important conclusion follows from this rapid survey. Moieties form a system. They possess and represent complementary properties that coincide and are opposed. Each assumes well-defined functions, shares a precise principle, and is permanently associated with a particular direction in space, with a season of the year, with a basic element of nature. These directions, seasons, and elements are always antagonistic. The personality of each moiety is indicated by its totem. The latter refers to one of the basic cosmic facts—directly, as is generally the case in North America, or through an animal intermediary that provides a convenient symbol for it, as often happens in Australia.

The tribe, like the entire universe, is the *product*[16] of the two moieties. It should be understood that the tribe *never* possesses the totem. It does not appear to be a substantive unit but the result of the fecund rivalry of its two active poles. The myths relating to the tribe's origin do not emphasize its unity but rather its duality. One is reminded of the Zuni tale, according to which everything originates from *two* pairs of different colored eggs. Australian legends are an exact parallel. The universe was created by mythical creatures called Nurali that possessed the forms of crows and eagle-hawks. It should be recalled that these are the totems of the moieties. They are depicted as constantly at war with one another. In the same way, the great tribal Gods, Bunjil, Daramulun, Baiame, are portrayed as the ancient totems of the moieties, elevated to the status of superior divinities. The crow and the eagle-hawk can easily be rediscovered in them, for they are in a state of perennial rivalry.

In the visible and the invisible, in the mythical and the real, the tribe does not appear to be a homogeneous unity but rather a totality that only exists and functions through the constant and fertile opposition of symmetrical units of objects and beings. These, in sum, embrace all nature and society without exception and thus, simultaneously, determine the structure of the *ordo rerum* and the *ordo hominum*.

One cannot assume that this interpretation is universally valid. At most, it can be established for totemistic societies. Its application to other areas is strictly limited. It does not apply to almost all of Africa and the greater part of Asia. In addition, the totemistic societies actually described very frequently manifest a very complex structure. They seem to derive, not from Gods but from several principles. To be sure, in most cases a vague dichotomy can be developed, but there is no cause to assume that it is systematic. It is sufficient for it to be duly observed, for its basic utility to be examined. It is preferable for it to be applied immediately to a large number of societies. As for other societies, if they only differ in the quantity of primary functional divisions, a simple adjustment, a *generalization* of the theory easily resolves the difficulty since its operative mechanism remains identical. Finally, if the latter is shown to be radically incompatible with it for a given group of societies, it is necessary for this purpose to resort to an interpretation specific to their organization.

At least, we can infer that the frequency of the Dakota type of nomenclature in kinship classifications affords an area of incomparable application to primitive exogomous divisions. Indeed, Lowie has particularly clarified the fact that the latter can hardly be explained as a vestige of the former. It can equally be asked if the succession of ruling power, embodying opposing qualities, ought not be related to an identical principle. In Cambodia, for example, the royal succession always alternates between a king of fire and a king of the water. In China, according to Granet, a time can be assumed when the chiefs of antagonistic groups alternated in power as the seasons changed. In every case, tradition shows that the government was ruled by a pair of rulers, the sovereign representing the heavenly quality, and his minister embodying the quality of earth. The second is subordinate to the first, but after having reached a certain age and after having acquired the heavenly quality by emerging victorious from ritual trials, he can force the sovereign to yield his throne to him.

SEXUAL, SEASONAL, AND SOCIAL SUBSTRATUM OF THE TOTEMIC QUALITIES

Durkheim and Mauss long ago observed that the notions of heaven and earth represent classificatory rubrics analogous to those they studied in totemistic societies. In effect heaven and earth correspond to male and female, light and darkness, ruler and subjects, etc. In particular, they found a link with space, time, and mythical creatures because the qualities of heaven and earth are in harmony with the qualities of the Yin and Yang principles, which in China dominate all social life and the universe. There is no type of opposition that they do not cover. Without doubt, this scholarly masterpiece is of definitive value in depicting the division of all the philosophic or vital data of a civilization. It must be viewed as the result of lengthy analysis.

Moreover, the social realities regarded by Granet as primary permit one to relate the principles of Yin and Yang with singular precision to those embodied in the moieties whose rivalry and collaboration assure the survival of the tribe. According to him, this bifurcation dominated the life of the ancient Chinese peasantry. It constituted an epoch that, in its entirety, appeared inextricably blended with and modeled after the opposition of Yin and Yang. The latter coincides with seasonal changes. Yin reflects the quality of winter, and Yang the quality of summer. The two governing categories originate from the equinoctial festivals, in the course of which on opposite sides of a river, men tilling the soil, working in the sun during the hot season, are in opposition to women weaving in their homes during the cold season. The two sexes thus inaugurate ritualistically, each in turn, their period of activity and subordination. Without doubt, Yang is male and Yin female. But numerous observations of Granet prove that this unqualified sexual antagonism is not the only opposition that contains the two principles. Perhaps it is not even the cause.

During the winter festivals, in fact, the farm laborers, gathered in the men's lodge, dance in order to promote the return of the warm season. These ceremonies involve "face to face opposition of the celebrants," and "alternation of movements." The dancers are aligned in two rival groups, one of which embodies the sun, warmth, summer, and Yang; the other, the moon, cold, winter, and Yin. *Women were excluded from these festivals.* Thus, the two principles and the two seasons that they represent are both impersonated by *men*. In this case, sexual antagonism is transferred to a second level. An attempt must be made to determine who performs in place of women. Granet suggests that the two groups of actors were composed of hosts and invited guests. One cannot but think of ritual tournaments and the athletic games of societies with moieties. The antithetical dances of the Chinese seasonal festivals seem an exact counterpart. They fulfil the same function and are based upon the same institutions. The one, perhaps, places men and women in opposition, but the other places rival and solidary clans face to face with each other, bound by an uninterrupted tradition of collective intermarriage, the structure of which Granet has also described, and which function exactly like the moieties of bipartite societies.

It is known that for a regular festival one of the dancing groups was composed of young boys, and the other of men. On this occasion the opposition between Yin and Yang did not coincide with that of the sexes, but with age levels. One must never forget that these are only *rubrics,* which in turn subsume the multiple contrasts encountered in nature and society, particularly that between the sexes and-between social groups. When the interplay of the moieties does not reflect the latter, the sexual contrast is apparent. Granet's work admirably demonstrates how this evolution is effected. The sexual aspect of Yin and Yang then assumes the dominant and almost exclusive position, so that at last it is discovered in later texts and permits the reconstruction of ancient Chinese civilization.

In addition, totemistic societies on occasion manifest a mystic and social opposition of the sexes. This is notably the case among the Kurnai where, independently of the clans, men are regarded as related to the emu-wren, and women to the superb warbler. These creatures have all the characteristics of totemic kings. It is expressly forbidden to kill and eat them. Each sex compels the other to respect the bird serving as its symbol, and any violation of the taboo leads to conflict between the sexes. These battles, sometimes bloody and sometimes reduced to mere games, are the ritual prelude to marriage. The same things happen as in the Chinese equinoctial festivals, in the course of which betrothals are also arranged. The emu-wren and the superb warbler are the functional equivalents of Yin and Yang.

If one thinks about it, it seems impossible for the social

dichotomy of the moieties to coincide with the physiological dichotomy of the sexes in that an exclusively masculine moiety is opposed to an exclusively feminine moiety. Such a division, which negates the blood tie too absolutely, would break every bond between brother and sister and would prevent the establishment of any kind of system of descent or family type. Also, the two basic principles of the universe and of society are embodied, on the one hand, in the sexes (concomitantly to assure biological fecundity); and, on the other hand, in the moieties (as factors in social harmony). Although this results in paradoxical overlapping, as evidenced by the facts, it is not disturbing if one views the world as populated by mysterious forces. Thus, certain men in the course of the festivals of the moieties can personify the female principle in the sexual tournaments.

In an extreme climate that makes seasonal change men's basic concern, the basic social antagonism is not determined by sex but by the seasons themselves, especially when the entire collective life is modified by climatic conditions, as in the vicinity of the Arctic Circle. Marcel Mauss has sufficiently clarified the magnitude of this transformation so that it need not be overly elaborated. Only the case of the Eskimo of Baffin-Land and Frobisher's Bay need be cited. There, as everywhere among these peoples, birth rites differ for children born in the summer from those born in the winter. But apart from this, all of one's life is influenced by the season of birth. The basic personality is also profoundly affected by it, deriving from one's sex, or in totemistic societies, one's moiety. Those born in wintertime are ptarmigans, and those born in summertime are eiders. They oppose each other in ritual tournaments, one tugging a rope inland, the other pulling it toward the seacoast. And from the type of encampment can be deduced which seasonal principle is dominant.

This system of summer and winter forms part of a system of correspondences no less complex than that reflected in the moieties or in Yin and Yang. Thus, a child born in *summer* drinks for its first meal a broth made from a terrestrial animal cooked in *fresh water*. A child born in *winter* drinks the broth made from an aquatic animal cooked in salt water. As in Australia, the classification embraces all of nature. All contact is forbidden between objects belonging to opposite seasons. Summer clothes are buried during the winter, and vice versa. The alternation of seasons determines the alternation of diets. The flesh of the salmon (a summer fish) can never be in contact with the flesh of a sea animal (winter fish). Hence, a system of taboos of intermixture is encountered that is very closely related to the food, hunting, etc., taboos of the totemistic societies, for the details of which one must turn to the work of M. Mauss. There is one difference, however. Here, the taboos are in force all year for each half of society, and there, half a year for the entire society. In one case, the division between the free and the guarded and between the profane and the sacred is tied to the social division into moieties and is based on a principle of reciprocity. In the other case, it follows the succession of the seasons and is based on the principle of rotation.

In every way, a bipartite conception of collective life and of the representation of the universe is observed. They are subordinate to the solidarity of the two rival principles in which the members of the tribe share and are in opposition. Now the antagonism of the seasons makes a transition to the first level, that of the sexes or of the moieties. Intermediate types occur, such as the sexual groups of the Kurnai and seasonal groups among the Eskimo of Baffin land. These diverse bases for opposition are not independent. They tend to overlap and be contradictory in that men are not born only in summer or women only in winter. Also, a mother's children may not be all male or all female. It is, therefore, necessary that one classificatory principle yield to the other. The primacy of this principle, attained in ways quite difficult to determine, is what gives the culture its basic pattern and explains the different functions of societies, such as those of the Chinese, Australian, or Eskimo type.

From this analysis, it must be recalled that the order of things and of men is frequently characterized by the combination of two principles—simultaneously and in varying proportion, social, sexual, and cosmic in nature. It is proper to

depict the totemic symbols of the moieties, therefore, and by
divination, of the clans, as *signs* manifesting the mysterious
qualities whose rivalry and collaboration preserve the universe and hold society together. The functioning of the moieties thus becomes meaningful, as do various totemic taboos,
particularly the one that carries so unfortunate a designation
as the taboo against incest.

THE PRINCIPLE OF RESPECT

This mechanism is governed by the principle of awe defined by Swanton. Each half of society corresponds to one of
the two complementary series, the union of which permits
and maintains the existence of the organized universe. It must
guard the preservation and integrity of the series that it represents and always keep it at the disposition of the social division in which the other series is embodied and which, for this
reason, must subsist with the co-operation of the first series.
Beings or objects grouped in the same mystic class are supposed to have in common a kind of substantive identity. Members of a clan share with their totem, and with everything classified under its rubric, a brotherhood that exerts pressure on
other groups, to the degree that it does not coincide with them.

The unity of the group is not territorial. It results from
the participation of all in an ideal category that is identified
with their intimate being, more deeply, for example, than
sex or hair color or eye color. Every object and every man is
imbued with this inalienable quality. It is inconceivable that
one may be deprived of it. The natives of the Trobriand Islands, reports Malinowski, ask the European visitor to which
class, of the four into which they have divided the universe
and themselves, he belongs. This quality, which essentially
affects the personality of each, is tatooed on their skins and
manifested to others by the clan name. Durkheim has properly
observed that in Australian societies tatooing constituted, in
the absence of fixed territory, permanent authority, or patrilineal kinship (the most frequent)—the only visible mark of

clan unity, the only effective symbol of the basic identity of its members.

In its absence, one's name has great significance. It is the integrating part of the personality. Those with the same name possess great solidarity and a kind of immortality. In ancient China, the family name, which is related to the name of the clan's place of origin (they must sound alike), determines the individual's destiny, initiates him into the social group, defines his obligations, and bestows its privileges upon him. "Personal name," writes Granet, "character or measure of life, witness of paternity, nuptial vow, maternal principle, title of power, and ancestral protector and *symbol* are roughly equivalent." This seems to read like the fundamental characteristics of totemic organization.

In fact, this would seem like a system of rights and duties in which each taboo corresponds to a complementary obligation that explains it. Killing and eating the totemic animal is forbidden the members of the clan, but members of other clans kill and eat it, just as the former do to the totemic animal of the latter. If it is strictly forbidden to marry women of one's own clan, it is because they are reserved for the men of the other clan, whose women are married to the men of the first clan. It is the same in everything. For that is the *principle of respect,* formulated by Swanton, and applied to the Tlingit and the Haida. Each moiety takes account of the other, whether on the ritualistic, alimentary, economic, juridical, matrimonial, or funeral levels.

Hertz has already observed that everything belonging to one moiety is *sacred and guarded* for its members, *profane and free* for members of the other. The sacred is thus bound most strictly to the order of the universe. It is its immediate expression and most direct consequence. The distinction between the sacred and profane reproduces and imitates that of social groups. Reciprocally, each furnishes the other with the essentials necessary for its survival—wives for reproduction, human victims for sacrifices, ceremonial or funeral services for its proper functioning—that the clan cannot provide for itself without defilement or peril.

At the time of obsequies among the Iroquois, or the Ca-
huilla of southern California, the active roles are assigned to
the moiety other than the one to which the deceased belonged.
In ancient China, the clan related to a certain animal, that is
to say, born the same year or in the course of the years homolo-
gous to the dozens of their animal eponyms, cannot officiate at
the burial of its members. It is necessary to seek the services of
those born under the influence of other animals.

This interdependence of the moieties in tribal ceremonies, in which each in its turn and to the advantage of the
other plays the active role and assumes responsibility, has often
been proved. It is part of the structure that Mauss has called
the *system of total vows,* the function of which he illustrated
with the example of the potlatch, and that he considers normal
in societies that have clans. "For," says he, "exogamy is wife
exchange among cognate clans. Rights and objects, religious
ritual, and miscellaneous rites are exchanged between clans
and their various generations as is evident, for example, among
the Warramunga of central Australia, where everything is
done by the moiety playing the active role, for the other
moiety, playing the role of the spectator." In fact, when the
men of the Uluuru moiety celebrate their festival, they are
decorated by those of the Kingilli moiety, who also prepare
the site, build the sacred mound around which the ceremony
unfolds, and play the role of spectators. The Uluuru render
the same services for them at their rituals.

DIETARY VOWS

The dietary factor in nature seems to be one of the important aspects of the system of total vows. Everything takes
place as if all the resources at the disposal of the tribes are divided among the moieties and the matrimonial classes. Spencer
and Gillen, among others, long ago observed that the totemic
system of the Aranda appears to be a vast economic organization. Each clan celebrates the ceremony called *intichiuma,*
in order to assure the food supply of the others. An equivalent
of this rite is encountered throughout most of the Australian

territory. While this festival is well known, it is necessary to retrace its rationale at this point.

It is important for the clan to regenerate the animal or vegetable species to which its existence is mystically bound and which is sacred to each of its members. Once this regeneration is obtained by appropriate rituals, there ensues a period during which the eating of the totemic species is strictly forbidden for the members of the clan concerned and restricted for the others. After that, they are free to hunt the animal or gather the plant. The products of this quest are assembled. Then, the chief of the totemic group tastes the food previously forbidden, and after him, all his clan aides taste it. The rest is sent, on condition of retaliation, to the men of the other clans, who can, from this moment on, dispose of it as they wish. In the northern tribes, the facts are even more significant. The men of the different clans bring and offer to their qualified representatives the totemic species whose *intichiuma* has just been celebrated. The latter refuse to taste it and say, "I have made it for you, and you can eat it freely."

In this way, one is certainly confronted with mutual dietary vows. Often the members of the clan abstain not only from eating the totemic animal, but also all the foods that are classified in the same rubric as that of which the totemic animal is the symbol. This is notably the case with the Mount Gambier tribe, where, for example, the clan of the venomless snake avoids eating this creature, and it also refrains from eating seals, eels, and all game or plants that they deem to possess the same nature.

Each moiety thus happens to be interested in seeing that the other executes the ceremonies correctly and observes strictly the concurrent taboos, in order to assure the reproduction and multiplication of their food supply. Among the Kaitish of central Australia, the duty of punishing violators of dietary taboos is assigned to men of the other moiety, who, in effect, are the ones who suffer the consequences of the violation. The system of moieties, with the taboo against eating the totemic species and the correlated obligation to consume

that belonging to the complementary group, is at the basis of
the economic order.

In China, the same principle is seen functioning analogously among allied and rival communities whose composition
determines and perpetuates the economic order. Grain and
cloth, according to Granet, were not originally objects of commerce or tribute, but "were used for antithetical vows," "were
yielded for retaliatory purposes." "The familial or sexual
group," he writes, "which, in threshing grain and weaving
cloth, incorporated something of its soul in it, and ate or wore
it only after having had it deconsecrated by an associated
group." So also do the members of the clan or of the moiety
who come to beg the chief of the opposing group to free their
food by being the first to taste it.

SEXUAL VOWS

The same principle of reciprocity applies to marriage.
The necessity for exogamy is not merely the positive side of
the taboo against incest. It is not only important to marry outside the group, but also to marry into another predetermined
group. One union is prohibited no less than the other is prescribed. Still, it is Marcel Granet who defines the phenomenon
most precisely by verifying that husband and wife are *as close
as they can be without reaching substantive identity*. The
latter is determined by the name, in addition, by belonging to
the moiety, to the cosmic principle that it embodies and whose
perpetuation it assures by its continuity. Marriage is a collective affair. In each generation, two groups exchange boys, if
matrilocal, and girls in the contrary situation. To recall the
felicitous phraseology of Granet, the spouses represent a par-
cel of hostages attesting to secular solidarity, the agency of the
rival group, the continually renewed pledges of an ancient alliance.

Union is prohibited between parallel cousins, those significantly called *sacred brothers* in other societies, but is obligatory for cross cousins. The result of this is that the same
word is used, on the one hand, for the paternal aunt and the

mother-in-law; on the other hand, for the maternal uncle and the father-in-law. In fact the traditional rule is that, when inheritance is through the mother's side, the young man marries his mother's brother's daughter and his father's sister's daughter, who have already been united by virtue of the same rule. A man cannot marry a woman unless he supplies another woman as compensation to the family of the one he is marrying, especially, as is natural, for the latter's brother. The conjugal union cannot be fertile unless it has taken place "between members of families that for the longest time past have maintained relationships followed by marriage."

The practice of exogamy between moieties can be defined in the same way, for between them also, marriages are universal and traditional. Each spouse received implies an obligation to furnish one in return, the child that she bears stimulates joy in her original group, assuring the continuity of the vital-flux, for the female is only lent to the other group. The young nephew is paired with his maternal uncle who lives far away, and whose rejuvenated and reinvigorated blood he represents. It is necessary to read Leenhardt's description of these relationships among the Kanakas of New Caledonia in order to perceive their true significance in all their complexity.

In every case, it is important to stress their character as obligatory vows kept in order by the exchange of the kind of mysterious money that the "sacred baskets" are. These represent for the maternal clan the value of every woman, of every source of life that they have sent to those with whom they are allied through matrimonial relationships. "It is the seal of the hope for children to come," writes Leenhardt, "for the daughters will return to get married in their mother's native village, and will take the place that she actually occupied as a girl." The going and coming of spouses between the moieties, the reverse circulation of the sacred baskets replacing them, make the basic fact of exogamy meaningful. It is the solidarity of the two social groups whose opposition is a combination of that of the sexes and of the generations.

Father and son, in effect, live together, but belong to opposite groups. The life of a man does not continue in his son,

but in the children of his sister, whom he has expatriated to
the complementary group. There, where they were born, the
boys remain, but the girls come back to their uncle's home to
marry his sons, and give him grandchildren. In this way, he
regains his flesh and blood. As for the boys, his nephews and
young vigor of his being, they remain in the antagonistic
group, in which they enjoy, in relation to the grandchildren,
the status of holders of life's blessings, that their uncle enjoyed
in relation to them. Thus, the vital fluid, at the heart of each
group, skips from grandfather to grandson, by passing through
the nephew by blood of the former, who is the maternal uncle
of the latter. Exogamy is nothing but this perpetual and obligatory exchange of females, which simultaneously sanctions
the solidarity and opposition of two social groups, two sexes,
and two successive generations.

As with the reciprocal dietary vows, it is the opposite
moiety that is the first to be concerned with the proper functioning of the institution. It is this moiety that is injured when
exogamy is violated and to whom compensation is due when
it has been basically frustrated in the principle of complementary existence, which returns a counterpart of what it
has supplied. Without this reciprocity, it cannot in effect assure its survival. "Daughters must be married outside the family, because rival families have rights to them," states Granet
à propos of Prince Huan of Ch'i, blamed by historians for having refused to marry his sisters and his aunts. Thus, he wished
to deprive the rival families of the hostage that the expatriated
spouse becomes. Perhaps he did more, for he violated the pact
assuring, on a secular level, the fertile union of the two opposing principles necessary to the prosperity of a race. Incest is
the business of rulers, since it is through incest, in conserving
the females in his family, that he upsets the balance to his
advantage, that he becomes pre-eminent.

Moreover, it has been observed that certain societies take
extreme precautions to avoid this breach of contract. Shortly
after their birth, children are sent to their mother's family and
are reared there until they become adults and marry their
cousins, but they are restored to their group only after their

sisters have been dispatched. This custom is called *fosterage*. To consider only the societies previously discussed, there is reason to assume that it was practiced in ancient China. In New Caledonia, a clear trace of it survives in the future husband's staying at the home of his maternal uncle, whose daughter is destined for him by the rules of exogamy, before being able to take her back to his village.

Sexual and dietary vows, and concerted ritual functions, are continuously interwoven with the solidarity of the groups that form the tribe on the human level, while their opposite qualities are invisibly combined to form the organic totality of the universe, simultaneously the material order and the order of mankind.

Sacred Laws and Sacrilegious Acts

SOLIDARITY OF THE MOIETIES

No attack upon this dual organization can be tolerated. The injury would have repercussions upon the entire universe by disturbing its order at a particular point. Therefore, it is protected by many taboos. The members of each group are forbidden to eat the food and marry the women who form a substantive unit with them and must be reserved for the opposite group.

In principle, each moiety and each clan can adopt a closed and autonomous economic system in place of the system of reciprocal gift exchange that operates in the majority of cases. In fact, sometimes in exceptional cases, societies are encountered in which it is permitted to marry women from one's own group and to eat the totemic food. Thus, the Toda moieties are endogamous, and among the Wakelbura, the members of the Mallera moiety eat the Mallera totem and the members of the Wuthera moiety eat the Wuthera totem. But this system does not assume the type of division that the other does. To consume only the food mystically assigned to one's group, and not to eat that belonging to the other, implies that the organizations are equal. In other areas of tribal life, the iden-

tical thing happens. For example, the funeral pyres are erected
by those associated with the moiety of the deceased. Dietary
autonomy corresponds to ceremonial autonomy. Autonomy
and interdependence are similarly based upon the allocation
of the free and the guarded, the profane and the sacred. The
problem is to understand the reasons why the first system is
so frequently preferred to the second.

Without doubt, a juxtaposition of independent groups
constitutes a bond, infinitely less capable of explaining the
functional unity of the tribe in all situations than the inter-
relationship of solidary groups. It must not be forgotten that
the totems of the moieties generally represent opposite qualities, the union of which is a source of fertility and regeneration. Also, it is important to recall that these qualities are impregnated in the essence of all the beings classified as part of
the social group in which they embodied, as are also all objects
subsumed under it. There is the same relationship between
these qualities as between male and female principles. Hence,
it appears to conform to the multiplication of species resulting
from the opposition of natural and sexual characteristics.

A marriage between individuals of the same "nature,"
that is to say, of the same social group, is regarded as destructive to the universal order, and is condemned to the most
wretched sterility, just as if it were a homosexual union. Thus
a Chinese adage, cited by Granet, becomes especially meaningful in declaring that the separation of the sexes is the basis for
exogamy. The aphorism appears absurd if taken literally,
exogamy defining the conditions for sexual union rather than
the separation of the sexes. But the foregoing allows one to
grasp the truth that it expresses. To wit, the complementariness of social groups in exogamous opposition is identical
with the complementariness of the sexes, possesses the same
significance, and has similar consequences. Thus, it manifests
not only the solidarity of the two moieties associated for political unity but, in addition, defines the necessary and sufficient conditions for the fertility of marriage.

From the union of individuals with the same nature, only
abortions or monsters can result. In China, the children of

spouses not related by blood but having the same name are regarded as necessarily degenerate. This is because the similarity of names is regarded as the sign of an identity of natures. Violators of the law of exogamy are punished in such a way that their spilt blood does not come in contact with the ground, lest it become sterile. The present belief that a marriage between near relations can only produce sickly and malformed children doubtless illustrates the antiquity of these ideas.

INCEST—AN ACT OF MYSTIC HOMOSEXUALITY

The violation of the rule of exogamy, therefore, not only represents, as defined by Thurnwald, "an infraction of the structure upon which the collective existence is based" but at the same time is the exact equivalent of homosexuality on a mystical level. It is an offense against the *ius* in injuring the opposing moiety, an offense against the *fas* in constituting an unnatural act. In fact it is very often so regarded. Nothing is more significant in this respect than Hardeland's dictionary of the Dyak language[17] that classifies it among *djeadjea* acts, which are unnatural and cause death by lightning. The *djeadjea* acts cited are typically, for example, the act "of giving a man or animal a name that is not his or its and is not proper to him or it or to say something about him that is contrary to his nature; for example, that a louse dances, or a rat sings, or a fly goes to war . . .; or to say of a man that he had a cat or another animal for a mother or wife." To bury any living animal and say, "I am burying a man"; (The fault lies not in the act of burial, but in what is said.) To skin a frog alive and say, "He has removed his cloak." Violation of the rule of exogamy is found to be linked with words of ill omen, sacrilegious in essence, that outrage the order of the universe and attack it merely in being pronounced.

In the same way, the pairing of different species of animals seems equivalent (still more significantly) to attempts at pairing animals of the same sex, for example, a sow mounting another sow. Such deviations can only disturb the universal order and would in fact, unless remedied in time, result in

earthquakes, floods, or droughts, and above all, in the sterility
of the soil. Such a correspondence exists between cause and
effect that, in societies with classification kinship where the
violation of exogamy is sometimes difficult to detect, the existence of incest is deduced from the appearance of an irregularity in the natural order, for example, the growth of two
pumpkins or two cucumbers on the same stem.

EATING THE TOTEM—A CANNIBALISTIC ACT

Incest is a special violation of the *ordo rerum*. It consists
of the impious and necessarily sterile union of two principles
symbolizing the same things. From this viewpoint, a violation
of the dietary taboo is exactly equivalent to it. In fact, just as
in marriage, a specifically polar relationship is required between the food and the eater for their mutual advantage. The
organism has no need of its own substance but of the one who
eats it. That is why the individual respects his totem and eats
the totem of the opposing group. To consume his own totem
is not nourishing but, on the contrary, would cause him to
languish and die of starvation, just as with a violation of
exogamy, for to eat it is monstrous, since devouring the flesh
of his totem, is the same as eating his own flesh. In the Banks
Islands, this act is regarded as explicitly cannibalistic. Also,
except for the case of ritual communion when it is important
for a member of the clan to renew the mystic principle by
which he lives, he does this only when pressed by dire necessity. Even then, he resorts immediately to expiatory rites.

To eat the totem and to violate the law of exogamy are
parallel offenses against the same law, which causes every
group to make a division between the sacred and the profane.
In the minds of the natives, they evoke the same qualms and
excite the same horror. They are often regarded as identical
and are designated by the same name. In New Britain, a Gun-
antuna old man explained to a missionary that the taboo
against eating the totem connotes "purely and simply" sexual
relations between the men of the totemic group, for carnal
relations are symbolized by the consumption of food. Inde-

pendently of this testimony, there are numerous reasons to think that in effect the sexual act is constantly equated with manifestions of voracity.

But what must be seen here is a strongly felt harmony, related to a particular conception of the universe, rather than a latent and unconscious identification of a general character. It is evident in the present case, as Lévy-Bruhl has very properly stressed. To eat totemic food or to marry a totemic woman are equivalent sins. In these situations, a *delinquent* act is committed by depriving the other group of what belongs to it. It is physiologically *harmful* and *sterile* (as against a normal union) and doubly *impious* because it violates the order of things. The offender, to begin with, defiles the mystic principle that he shares and all its manifestations that he should respect.

The parallel is obvious. Without doubt, the violator of the dietary taboo has become cannibalistic, just as the violator of the exogamic taboo has become homosexual, for the two acts strictly correspond and are analogous. In both cases, it is contradictory to the mystic quality one ought to respect. It is an act of violence against that which embodies the sacred. The act has two simultaneous characteristics, for it is a *Missbraucht,* an abnormal abuse, brutal rape. It is a kind of sacrilege and implies a major defilement. Perhaps nothing can make this complex more meaningful than a verse from *The Suppliants* that recalls an old proverb, a survival from the long-dead past, but whose use by Aeschylus in this context is remarkably appropriate. "How can a bird that has eaten another bird remain pure?" asks Danos. It is significant that this maxim is used to condemn a sacrilegious marriage, which even death cannot expiate. It is a union regarded as offensive to the cosmic order, the *thémis,* and is described as "the desire of enemies related by blood, who bring defilement to their clan."

MURDER OF A MEMBER OF THE CLAN—PARTIAL SUICIDE

Associated with the violation of dietary or sexual taboos is a third crime—the murder of a member of the group. To

eat the totem, to possess a female, and to kill a man of the same
totemic group, are three aspects of the same crime, of the same
attack upon the mystic integrity of the clan. Food, women, and
victims must be sought outside the group. Inside the community everything is sacred and commands respect. The hand
should not be used to satisfy a gluttonous, erotic, or murderous
desire.

In New Britain, where each tribe is divided into exogamous moieties, the same word is used to designate one who
kills or eats another man as for one who violates the rule of
exogamy. He is not responsible for merely a homicide, but he
weakens, mutilates, and injures the commonweal, the quality
diffused through the social and cosmic domain of which he
is part. Besides, the group would be no less weakened, mutilated, or injured if it executed the offender. In doing this, the
members of his moiety (just as do the natives of Samoa) appear
to "commit suicide," to agree to a kind of *suicide partiel,* according to Levy-Bruhl's cogent phrase. So in most cases they
forego executing the murderer. It so happens that he may
not even be disturbed. Among the Eskimo, every accidental
homicide is esteemed. At worst, the criminal is merely banished from the group in order that the contagion from his
defilement should not spread. He is declared *sacred.* He is
expelled, as a *violater of exogamy,* on a boat without sails, rig-
ging, or oars. In each instance, care is taken not to make a direct attempt upon his life.

Now it may be seen that Robertson Smith's definition of
an Arabic clan ("the group in which there is no blood vengeance") is nothing else but the counterpart of the definition
of the clan as the group in which marriage is forbidden. Marriage and vengeance only take place between clans or moieties.
They form equally solid bonds and by the same token constitute *blood relationships,* one corresponding to the state of
peace, the other to the state of war, but completely symmetrical. Murders are as strictly regarded as marital unions, for the
supplying of spouses is equivalent to the avenging of the slain.
Homicides and weddings are viewed as pledges that must be
honored, and in the same manner cause an imbalance that can

only be ended by the appropriate counterpart. There must be murder for murder, spouse for spouse.

Granet has very strongly emphasized this concordance by observing that in China neither feuds nor marriages are possible between relatives. "Wars of vengeance," he remarks, "just like sexual conflicts, are the means by which those who do not share the same name or nature are likened and allied, and approach or oppose each other." Between rival and associated moieties, blood calls for blood. If it has been spilt in one moiety by an act of the other, the members of the former, their very existence under attack, cannot rest until they have obtained, by an equivalent vow, the blood that will appease the dead and above all satisfy the law of equilibrium which dominates the relationships of complementary groups.

The harmony that prevails among them is thus accomplished by a series of dissymmetries, alternately exposed and erased by the continuous exchange of ceremonies, women, and food that has been described. It is evident that murders are placed among the disequilibria whose creation and destruction regularly manifest the solidarity of the moieties. They permit to exist the union of its mobility, its rhythm of growth and decline, its abruptness, and its spring, with the essentially static reality, stopped by the order of things, that is thus adapted to the same process of becoming. After the assassination of Agamemnon by Clytemnestra, the mover of vengeance invoked by Electra is the *nemesis of death*, that is to say, the cosmic force that tends to avenge every attack upon the universal law, and a concrete emanation of which, specific and exacting, relieves the soul of the deceased and claims satisfaction for it, until the spilling of the enemy's blood restores, through just reckoning, the system of relationships for men and things.

THE TRIBE—A LIVING UNITY

Reciprocal gifts of food, exchange of spouses, and payment of blood debts form an impeccable pattern attesting to the proper functioning of tribal life. Such would appear to be the typical structure from which taboos, in societies with moieties, derive. Taboos define the sphere of the sacred in man's life and limit the extent of his free or profane activity. The moieties represent the equilibrium and solidarity of two principles whose division creates order, union, and fertility. The names they bear are symbols that mark the opposition of their respective qualities—heaven and earth, earth and water, water and fire, black bird and white bird.

Hence, nothing can combat the category of the pair, whose influence is clearly evident in primitive thought. The native does not conceive a unity, for everything that is exists in his eyes as one of a pair. Leenhardt has shown this very well in the case of the Kanakas of New Caledonia. Uncle and nephew, husband and wife, form a pair that constitute true unity, the first term in numbering, with one over the other, from which *fractions* begin. The isolated individual, springing from an elementary duality, is a *lost* and *errant* being. He does not form a unity, but an incomplete fragment of a living unity. The Kanaka does not know the indefinite article. He does not say *a* house, but the *other* house, for no being or object possesses independent existence. Each *one* is felt to be the complement of an *other* in a dyad, just as each moiety is complementary to the other in the society.

The union of the sexes in marriage conveys an immediate and perfect image, a true and complete likeness of the concept of the couple. From this model can be understood all social life. Each moiety brings the other what it lacks in various circumstances. Moreover, the principle incarnated in each, and which is embodied in its members, not only must be united with the opposing principle but must be strengthened and invigorated in its essence. On the one hand, it is necessary to seek its complementary entity, to make all creation possible; on the other, to stay away from it, in order not to corrupt its own qualities. On the one hand it is necessary to respect whatever possesses the same quality as it does; on the other, to steep oneself in it, to feed upon it in order to reinforce this quality in oneself. The Aranda of the water totem must make only moderate use of this liquid, in respectful and deferential manner. However, when it is raining, he must leave his hut that provides shelter from the elements and expose himself for a long time to the beneficent action of the animating principle that strengthens him as it pours down upon him.

Hierarchy and Lèse-Majesté

As a consequence of the increasing complexity of society, it happens that the interplay of the moieties loses in importance by contrast to organization into specialized groups. In this case, the dominance of the notion of the couple is lost, and with it, the feeling of reciprocity in which services rendered and received are in equilibrium. Evidence of solidarity in which each, indispensable to the other, gives as much as he takes, is no longer observed. The tendency that enables each group to keep its integrity alone persists. Then it is no longer important to maintain its vital quality intact in order to put it at the exclusive disposition of the other moiety of the social group, but to exalt it and try to assure its supremacy over the other principles whose joint action perpetuates the existence and welfare of the tribe. There is no longer any thought of preserving, together with the opposing group, a perfect equilibrium that each is most interested in maintaining. Rather, each aspires to increase its prestige and become dominant.

THE GENESIS OF POWER

A principle of individuation is affirmed in place of the principle of respect. The symmetrical relationship between the moieties is succeeded by an unstable state of rivalry between the traditional clans. The latter are gradually transformed into confraternities specialized in terms of such social function as each of them is privileged and obligated to assume. From this time on, the functioning of the society reposes in co-operation—a group co-operation whose principles, operating in concert for the harmony of the universe, seek less to balance one another than to become dominant, to preserve this dominance once obtained, to have it recognized as right when in fact it is most in dispute.

Among the Zuni of North America, bipartite organization, we have seen, scarcely is ever found except in mythical recollection. The contemporary culture only has knowledge of confraternities, recruited mainly from the clans belonging to the same geographic regions as the functions they perform. Thus, the northern clans are affiliated with the warrior societies, those of the west with sacerdotal societies, those of the east with the dancing societies, and those of the south with agricultural societies and associations of medicine men. In China, Granet notes a parallel substitution for the ancient dichotomy, of special groups whose qualities are realized in the form of winds and who contribute "in dancing, in jousting, and in competing for prestige, to the preservation of a cosmic order."

It is useless to recapitulate at this point all the various possible types of evolution of social organization, even more useless to pass in review the various types of social structure present in the world. The conclusion for the study of the sacred drawn from each analysis would always be the same, i.e., the presence of a hierarchy, the exercise of sovereignty, both clothed in dignity, invulnerable, stunning, rendering sacrilegious every error committed with regard to them.

It matters little that the specialized confraternities assumed the form of closed, hereditary castes arranged according to a fixed order of precedence. It matters little that the will to co-operation has been completely eliminated by the will to power. Often, as Davy has shown, to be witness to respect is to become the means of imposing respect. To be most generous in the influential distribution of wealth and food ends by "giving to the service rendered the form of a defiance of the power to recognize it." These measures have culminated in establishing the superiority of one clan in the tribe, of one individual in the clan. A chief is needed to assemble the treasures and conduct the ceremony in the course of which he bestows a scornful and self-interested gift upon whomever he pleases, and by this means seizes advantage and establishes sovereignty. In these matters, any genetic reconstruction is dubious, allows of contradiction, and—sooner or later—seems destined for refutation.

Under these conditions, it would seem better to accept personal power as a new datum, without trying unduly to derive it from a prior state. To be sure, it must be remembered that the same ceremonies (construction of the long house, erection of funeral platforms, initiation of young men, etc.) in which, among the Tlingit for example, solidarity and the equilibrium of the moieties are manifested, are, among the Kwakiutl for example, those in which superiority is proved by ostentatious expenditure impossible to pay or *render* in return.[18] Nothing is changed in the ritual, but the clan totems have become the coats-of-arms of the leaders of the contest, the personal emblems of the chiefs who inherit and traffic in them, who give and receive them, who lose and win them, thus gathering on their heads the mystic qualities and prestige conferred by possessing them.

THE FACT OF POWER—AN IMMEDIATE DATUM

It is important to pause to consider the naked fact of power. Whatever may be the roads by which personal influence becomes fixed in recognized authority, it is appropriate to note the irreducible character, the intimate nature of power. Here, one encounters a notion no less immediate, primary, and unbreakable than the opposition of the sexes, in the image of which the reversible division of the sacred and profane, in societies with moieties, appears to be formed. It manifests an *ananke stenai*[19] equally imperative.

Obviously, that is not to say that sexual polarity or the relationship between commander and subordinate, which defines power, cannot in any case be explained. Rather, the one who takes it into account elevates it to a general conception of the universe, and it passes beyond the category of a special problem. It is preferable to be content with noting the absolute uniqueness of the reality of power and stressing the strict

continuum almost identifying its nature with that of the
sacred.

Independent of its origin and its point of application, in
all its imaginable variations as it is exercised over things and
men, power seems like the gratification of a desire. It manifests
the omnipotence of speech, whether commandment or incanta-
tion. It causes orders to be executed. It is presented as an invisible, weighty, and irresistible quality that is manifested in
the chief as the source and principle back of his authority.
This quality, which compels obedience to his injunctions, is
the same as that which gives wind the ability to blow, fire the
ability to burn, and a weapon the ability to kill. It is designated, in various ways, by the Melanesian word *mana* and its
numerous American equivalents. The man who possesses
mana is the one who knows how to make others obey.

Power, like the sacred, seems to be an external sign of
grace, of which the individual is the temporary abode. It is
obtained through investiture, initiation, or consecration. It
is lost through degradation, indignity, or abuse. It benefits
from the support of the entire society, which constitutes its
depository. The king wears the crown, sceptre, and purple reserved for the Gods. He has guards to protect him. He executes
all types of coercion capable of forcing the rebellious to submit. But it must be pointed out that these means do not explain as much as they demonstrate the efficacy of power. To
the degree to which people regard them as powerful, or consider them able to subjugate, or reveal reasons for being afraid,
it is unnecessary to explain the motives for complaisance and
docility.

Whatever the kind of power—civil, military, or religious
—it is only a consequence of consent. The discipline of an
army is not a product of the power of the generals but of the
obedience of the soldiers. At every level of the hierarchy, the
problem is posed in the same terms. From field marshal to
corporal, each is powerless if his subordinates, more numerous
and better armed, refuse to obey their orders. La Boétie[20] has
shown very well that it is not so much a type of servitude as
it is voluntary. For spying upon men, the tyrant has only their

eyes and ears, and for oppressing them, only the loan of their arms.

THE SACRED CHARACTER OF POWER

It is important to emphasize this paradox of power, the primacy of the relationship that unites the dominated to the dominator. It is based on the effective interplay of different levels of energy that automatically causes one to submit to the other and gives one immediate influence over the other. The basic privilege of personal prestige already establishes this polarity and sheds light upon its presence and role. It is a relationship between one who is so endowed and exercises it and one who is so deprived and submits to it. The term "power" is astrological in origin. It designates the zodiacal constellation that comes over the horizon at the moment of an individual's birth.

This is a significant fact. It shows how one tends to objectify, to project to the stars, in a word, to divine the source of power. For the most pressing reasons, this process takes place when the privileges of authority do not seem like personal qualities, unstable and obscure, fragile and vulnerable, but as a prerogative inherent in a social funtion, assured, evident, recognized, and in an atmosphere of respect and fear. Every king is God, descended from God, or ruler by the grace of God. He is a sacred personage. It is consequently necessary to isolate him and to construct watertight compartments between him and the profane. His person harbors a holy force that creates prosperity and maintains the order of the universe. He assures the regularity of the seasons and the fertility of the soil and women. The virtue of the blood that he spills guarantees the annual reproduction of edible species of plants and animals. His conduct is regulated to the minutest detail. He must not bungle or misuse his divine power. In that event, he is held responsible for famines, droughts, epidemics, and floods. He alone possesses sanctity sufficient to commit the sacrilege necessary to deconsecrate the harvest, so that his subjects may have free use of it.

This sanctity causes him to be dreaded. All that he touches can only be used by him. Similarly, the vessel from which he has eaten and the clothing that he has worn become dangerous for others and cause the loss of their possessions. It is sufficient for a Polynesian chief to name an object after a part of his body and he becomes its owner, imbuing it with a deadly power. He can also consecrate (declare *taboo*) a river or a forest. Traffic there is then forbidden, and no profane or useful act can henceforward be performed there.

The possessor of such power is himself kept in splendid and strict isolation. Contact with him would strike down the imprudent one who touches him. Anyone who, through ignorance or inadvertance, places his hand upon a chief's property, must immediately be disinfected and freed from an emanation too powerful for him. Until that is done, he cannot make use of his hands. If he is hungry, he must be fed by someone else or eat like an animal, tearing at the food with his teeth. Otherwise, his hand, impregnated with the chief's sanctity, would communicate it to the food, and in eating it, would introduce the chief's sanctity to his wretched organism, which could not tolerate it, and he would die.

Similarly, the chief is addressed only indirectly. In China, the expression [*those who are*] *at the bottom of the steps* [*of the throne*] has become a simple equivalent of *Your Majesty*. Again, one does not look at the sovereign's face. The impure breath exhaled in profane speech and the debilitating emanation from the gaze of an inferior would defile and weaken the divine quality of the ruler.

In addition, power confers new qualities upon the person. It sanctifies him no less than the priesthood. The one who accepts or seizes it becomes pure. His life is changed. If before that it had been debauched or criminal, it now becomes ascetic and exemplary. History opposes Octavius to Augustus, and poetry opposes Don Carlos to Charles the Fifth. This is not merely an imaginary need. The one upon whom all gifts depend, whose existence is the venerated model and the support of all others, must necessarily possess all the virtues and all greatness. One lends to him without bargaining for what he has not.

It is not enough merely to shelter the chief from the intrusion of the profane. All his life, he must be remote from the common condition. The use of the precious is reserved for him, and, the use of the mean is forbidden to him. Routine actions that are permitted to his subjects are forbidden to him, or if he performs them, it is in a different way. It is inconceivable that a sacred personage should work at a fatiguing or vulgar occupation. The ideal is that he do nothing wrong, that he reign but not govern. The simple and regular diffusion of his holy energy renders his beneficent influence efficacious. He must not eat what others eat, or do what they do. Conversely, his special diet is prohibited to his subjects. Even his sexual behavior is unique. Incest, forbidden to the people, is expected of royal or noble families. Besides, in order that sacred and profane blood should not be mixed, it is important, in these matters too, to differentiate carefully between the chief's law and that of his subjects.

EQUILIBRIUM AND HIERARCHY

Again, the sacred and profane seem complementary. What is sacrilege for some is holy rule for others, and vice versa. The same principle of division is operative between king and subjects as between moieties. But, in these cases, dichotomization implies equilibrium, is based on mutual respect, assigns the same rights and duties to each, allows or forbids symmetrical actions to all—in a word, institutes reciprocal relations between the sovereign and his people, between the noble and the pariah castes, and the relationships are regularized and set in a hierarchy.

The rules are not mutually valid. The complementary side of each right is not a right for the other party but an equivalent duty. *Lèse-majesté* is henceforward regarded as a great sacrilege. It is unilateral, and can only be committed by one who is at the bottom against one who is on top. The same act when committed by the one at the top against the one on bottom is not regarded as a crime but as a favor, not as sin that corrupts but as grace that absolves.

In Polynesia, one who touches a sacred personage, swells up and dies. To ward off the death that awaits him, the offender or the rash one has no other recourse than to persuade a chief to let himself be touched by him. Thus the sanctity is led back to an organism able to support it. The malignant effect of the improper and derogatory contact is destroyed by the acceptable and permitted contact. The Nubians[21] of East Africa cannot enter the royal hut without dying, but to escape this peril, it suffices that the monarch consent to touch their uncovered left shoulders lightly with his hand. This gesture sanctifies them, and permits them to penetrate the consecrated place without fear.

The consequences are generally the opposite when the king touches or names the subject, or when the subject touches the king. That is because to touch and name are presented as prerogatives of power or as demonstrations of superiority. In naming an object or a being, it is evoked and forced to appear and almost to obey, for it is constrained to present itself. To name is always to call, already to order. Similarly, in placing a hand upon a thing or person, it is subjugated, used, and transformed into an instrument. The *manus iniectio* is an expropriation, an acquisitive act, a laying of violent hands upon something that has been seized.

From king to subject, the manifestation of superiority follows the order of things. It constitutes a benediction. From subject to king, it runs counter to universal law and constitutes a sacrilege that disturbs it. A rising stream of offerings from the lowest to the highest levels of the social hierarchy and a descending stream of favors from the highest to the lowest levels is substituted for the ever recurrent confrontation, for the ceaselessly renewed exchange that, in turn, binds and rebinds and the antithetical groups of tribes with moieties. Power also places the society in a polar relationship. But the model for the latter is no longer based upon the relationship of man and wife, but of father and son. This type of relationship does not imply collaboration as much as subordination.

For the rest, the two relationships are not mutually exclusive but are combined in varying proportions. Subordination already exists between husband and wife. Conversely, an equilibrium tends to be established between king and people, and between lord and body of liege men. The "good" sovereign applies himself to preserve it, but the tyrant—almost always considered as disturber and transgressor of the typical order of the universe, as author of troubles, disorders, and riots—is deemed to have broken it.

The monarch does not have any fewer duties toward the social group than the latter has toward him. Society is based upon their co-operation. In China, the prince is *Yang*, the masses are *Yin*. Thus, their relationship is complementary. Moreover, it happens that the prestige of an individual or the privilege of a minority is counterbalanced by that of the greater number, and its influence is balanced. Between the king and the entire organized populace exists, as between moieties, mutual respect that is like a testimony to alliance, esteem, and recognition, that obligate two parties, equal in dignity, and indispensable to each other.

On the contrary, between the sovereign and each of his subjects, it is the relationship of authority that matters—the relationships of protector and protege in one sense, of master and servant in another. The kind of respect exists between them that implies enfiefment, either with consent or by imposition. All etiquette manifests it, and it is presented as a solemn avowal of dependency, or deferential and submissive homage, owing to the noble by the serf, to the suzerain by the vassal, to the old man by the young man, to the master by the disciple, to the initiator by the initiate, to the initiate by the profane, so aptly named.

Of these relationships, some are or tend to become hereditary, others constitute transitory states but evolve in the course of time. The young man becomes an adult, the son becomes a father in his turn, but without ceasing to be a son to his own father, just as the young man never catches up to the one who is older than he. Also, all these relationships comprise an irreversible, linear order of the universe, in contrast to the circular and balanced order of societies with moieties. The crime of *lèse-majesté* thus is ranged alongside of sacrilegious acts (use of sacred food or forbidden women) that attack the universal order and that provoke a break, a disturbance or an hiatus in the functioning of the society.

CONSERVATION AND CREATION

In both cases, virtue consists in remaining *in the order,* keeping in one's *own* place, not leaving one's station, keeping to what is permitted, and not approaching what is forbidden. Having done this, one also keeps the universe ordered. That is the function of taboos in ritual prescriptions. "Rites," says Li-K'uei, "prevent disorder, just as dams prevent floods."

But time erodes dams, and the functioning of a mechanism wears away and soils its parts. Man grows old and dies, renewed, it is true, in his descendants. Nature at the approach of winter loses its fertility and seems to die. It is necessary to recreate the world, to rejuvenate the system. Taboos can only prevent its accidental end. They are incapable of saving it from its inevitable destruction, from its beautiful death. They slow its decline, without being able to stop it. The moment comes when rebuilding is necessary. A positive act must assure a new stability to the order. A facsimile of creation is needed to restore nature and society. That is what the festival provides.

Chapter IV—THE SACRED AS TRANS-GRESSION: THEORY OF THE FESTIVAL

THE EXHILARATION OF THE FESTIVAL[22] IS OPPOSED TO OR-dinary life, occupied as the latter is with daily tasks and hemmed in with a system of taboos and precautions in which the maxim *quieta non movere* maintains the order of the universe. If only its external aspects are considered, the festival demonstrates identical characteristics on all levels of civilization. It connotes a large conglomeration of moving and boisterous people. These massed gatherings eminently favor the creation and contagion of an exalted state that exhausts itself in cries and movement and that is incited to uncontrollably abandon itself to the most irrational impulses. Even today, when attenuated and infrequent festivals grow out of the gray background symbolizing the monotony of contemporary existence and seem scattered, crumbling, and almost submerged, there can still be distinguished in these festivals some miserable vestiges of the collective euphoria that characterized the ancient celebrations. In fact, the disguises and audacious acts permitted at carnival time, the drinking and dancing in the streets on July 14, attest to the same and continuing social necessity. There is no festival, even on a sad occasion, that does not imply at least a tendency toward excesses and good cheer. The burial feast in rural areas is an example. In times past or at present, the festival is always characterized by dancing, singing, dining, and drinking. It is necessary to eat to the point of exhaustion or illness. That is the very law of the festival.

The Festival, Resort to the Sacred

In civilizations described as primitive, the contrast is much more evident. The festival lasts several weeks, or several months, punctuated by rest periods of four or five days. It often takes several years to re-amass the amount of food and wealth ostentatiously consumed or spent, and even destroyed and wasted, for destruction and waste, as forms of excess, are at the heart of the festival.

The festival ends voluntarily, in a frenetic and orgiastic way, with nocturnal debauchery involving noise and movement while the crudest instruments are beaten as a rhythmic accompaniment to the dance. According to the description of an observer, the human mass, swarming, undulating, and stamping the ground, pivots and sways about a center pole. The movement increases as a result of many stimuli. It is augmented and intensified by whatever enhances it—the clash of spears on shields, guttural chants of a rhythmic nature, the jerking and promiscuity of the dance. Violence erupts spontaneously. From time to time quarrels break out. The combatants are separated, lifted up by strong arms and balanced in cadence until they are calmed. The dance is not interrupted. Couples suddenly leave the dance to have sexual relations in the surrounding woods, returning to take their place in the frenzy that continues until morning.

It is understood that the festival, being such a paroxysm of life and cutting so violently into the anxious routine of everyday life, seems to the individual like another world in which he feels sustained and transformed by powers that are beyond him. His daily activity—food gathering, hunting, fishing, or cattle raising—can only occupy his time and provide for his immediate needs. Doubtless it requires his attention, patience, and skill, but more profoundly, he lives by recalling the festival and awaiting another, since the festival signifies for him, in memory and desire, a time of intense emotion and a metamorphosis of his being.

ADVENT OF THE SACRED

It is to Durkheim's honor that he recognized the splendid illustration of the distinction between the sacred and profane that festivals afford, in contrast to working days. In effect, they oppose an intermittent explosion to a dull continuity, an exalting frenzy to the daily repetition of the same material preoccupations, the powerful inspiration of the communal effervescence to the calm labors with which each busies himself separately, social concentration to social dispersion, and the fever of climactic moments to the tranquil labor of the debilitating phases of existence. In addition, the religious ceremonies forming part of the festival agitate the souls of the believers. If the festival is the time of joy, it is also the time of anguish. Fasting and silence are required before the festival starts. Habitual taboos are reinforced, and new restrictions are imposed. Debauchery and excess of all kinds, the solemnity of the ritual, and the severity of the previous restrictions are equally united to make the environment of the festival an exceptional world.

In reality, the festival is often regarded as the dominion of the sacred. The day of the festival, the Sabbath, is first of all a day consecrated to the divine, on which work is forbidden, on which one must rest, rejoice, and praise God. In societies in which festivals are not diffused throughout one's working life but grouped into a true *festival season,* the point at which the latter in fact constitutes the period of sacred pre-eminence can be seen even better.

Mauss's study of Eskimo society provides the best examples of the violent contrast between the two kinds of life, always meaningful for peoples where climate or the nature of their economic organization condemns them to prolonged inactivity for part of the year. In winter, Eskimo society contracts. Everything is done or takes place communally, as against the summer when each family, isolated in its tent in an almost desert-like vastness, finds its food separately with nothing intervening to reduce the role of individual initiative. In contrast to the summertime, almost entirely secular, winter seems a time "of continuous religious exaltation," a protracted festival. Among the American Indians of the far north, social organization varies no less seasonally. There also, the concentration of winter succeeds the dispersion of summer. Clans disappear and give way to religious confraternities, which then perform the great ritual dances and organize tribal ceremonies. It is the epoch for the transmission of myths and rites, a time in which spirits appear to novices and initiate them. The Kwakiutl have a saying, "in summer, the sacred is on the bottom, and the profane is on top; in winter, the sacred is on top, the profane on the bottom." It could not be phrased more clearly.

It has been demonstrated that the sacred, in ordinary life, is expressed almost exclusively through taboos. It is defined as "the guarded" or "the separate." It is placed outside common usage, protected by restrictions destined to prevent any attack upon the order of the universe, any risk of upsetting it or introducing any source of disturbance into it. It seems essentially *negative*. This is, in fact, one of its basic characteristics, one most often observed in ritual taboos. Hence, the sacred period of social life is precisely that in which rules are suspended, and license is in order. Without doubt, a ritualistic meaning can be denied to the excesses of the festival, and they can be considered merely as *discharges of energy*. "In this way, one is outside the restraints of the ordinary conditions of existence," writes Durkheim, "and one is so adjusted to it that he places himself beyond the bounds of ordinary morality." To be sure, the unrestrained movement and exuberance of the festival corresponds to a kind of detumescent impulse. Confucius took this into account when he said, in justifying the merrymaking of Chinese peasants, that it is unnecessary "to always keep the bow taut, without ever unbending it, or always unbent without ever stretching it." The excesses of collective ecstasy certainly *also* fulfil this function. They arise as a sudden explosion after long and strict repression. But this is only one of their characteristics, less an assurance of their reason for being than their physiological mechanism. This characteristic must be cathartic. In fact, the natives see in them the magical efficacy of their festivals. They attest, in advance, to the success of the ritual and thus indirectly give promise of fertile women, rich harvests, brave warriors, abundant game, and good fishing.

EXCESS, AN EROSIVE REMEDY

Excess constantly accompanies the festival. It is not merely epiphenomenal to the excitement that it engenders. It is necessary to the success of the ceremonies that are celebrated, shares in their holy quality, and like them contributes to the renewal of nature or society. In reality, this seems to be the goal of the festivals. Time passes and is spent. It causes one to age and die, it is that which *wears away*.[23] The Greek and Iranian root from which the word is derived has the same meaning. Each year vegetation and social life are renewed as nature inaugurates a new cycle. All living things must be rejuvenated. The world must be created anew.

The latter comprises a *cosmos* ruled by universal order and functioning according to a regular rhythm. A sense of proportion and a rule maintain it. Its law is that everything has *its own* place, that every event happens in *its due* time. This explains the fact that the sole manifestations of the sacred may be in the form of taboos, which protect against anything capable of threatening the cosmic regularity, or of expiations and reparations for all that can disturb it. It tends toward immobility, for any change or innovation may be perilous to the stability of the universe, whose development one wishes to control so as to destroy the chance of death. But the seeds of its destruction reside in its very functioning, which accumulates waste and induces the erosion of its mechanism.

There is nothing that this law may not subsume, defined and confirmed as it is by all experience. The very health of the human body requires the regular evacuation of its "defilement," urine and feces and menstrual blood for the female.

In the end, however, old age weakens and paralyzes it. In the same fashion, nature each year passes through a cycle of growth and decline.

Social institutions are not exempt from this alternation. They must also be periodically regenerated and purified of the poisonous waste matter that represents the ill-omened residue left by each act performed for the good of the community. Necessary as it may be, it is evident that it involves some defilement for the officiator who assumes responsibility for it, and by extension, for the entire society. Thus, the Gods of the Vedic pantheon seek a creature to which they can transfer the impurity that they contract by spilling blood in the course of the sacrifice. This type of purging is generally effected by expelling or putting to death a scapegoat charged with all the sins that have been committed, or a personification of the old year which must be replaced. It is necessary to expel evil, weakness, and erosion, notions that more or less coincide. In Tonkin, rites are performed with the explicit goal of eliminating the impure residue from each event, particularly from acts of authority. One seeks to neutralize the irritation and the malevolence of those whom the government has condemned to death for treason, rebellion, or conspiracy. In China, they pile up refuse, the daily waste matter of domestic living, near the door of the house, and it is carefully disposed of during the New Year's festivals. Like all defilement, it contains an active principle that results in prosperity when properly utilized.

The elimination of the waste matter accumulated by every organism's functioning, the annual liquidation of sins, and the expulsion of the old year are not sufficient. They only serve to bury a dying and sullied past, *which has had its day,* and which must give way to a virgin world whose festival is destined to hasten its arrival. Taboos are demonstrably powerless to maintain the integration of nature and society. They are unable to restore it to its early youth. Rules do not possess any inherent principle capable of reinvigorating it. It is necessary to invoke the creative quality of the Gods, to return to the beginning of the world, and to resort to the powers which at that time transformed chaos into cosmos.

THE PRIMORDIAL CHAOS

In fact, the festival is presented as a re-enactment of the first days of the universe, the *Urzeit*, the eminently creative era that saw all objects, creatures, and institutions become fixed in their traditional and definitive form. This epoch is none other than the one in which the divine ancestors, whose story is told in mythology, lived and moved. The myths of the Tsimshian of North America are precisely distinguished from other legendary tales by the fact that they take place in this time long-past, when the world had not yet assumed its present form.

The character of this mythical dream-time[24] has been the subject of an excellent study by Levy-Bruhl, with special reference to the Australians and Papuans. Each tribe has a special term to designate it. It is the *altjira* of the Aranda, the *djugur* of the Aluridja, the *bugari* of the Karadjeri, the *ungud* of the peoples of northwest Australia, etc. These words often designate, at the same time, dreams and, in a general way, anything that seems unusual or miraculous. They serve to define a time in which "the exception was the rule." The expressions used by observers all seem to illustrate this aspect of the primordial age. According to Fortune, this mythical time is one in which "life and natural history begin." It is located simultaneously at the *beginning* and *outside* of evolution. Elkin remarks that it is no less present or future than past. "It is a state as well as a period," he significantly writes.

Basically, the mythical time is the origin of the other and continuously re-emerges by causing everything that is manifestly disconcerting or inexplicable. The supernatural is always discovered lurking back of the natural, and it ceaselessly tends to manifest itself in this sphere. The primordial age is described with singular unanimity in the most diverse areas. It is the ideal place for metamorphoses and miracles as nothing has yet been stabilized, no rule pronounced, and no form fixed. Whatever has long been impossible, was then feasible. Objects would disappear, canoes would fly through the air, men would be transformed into animals, and vice versa. They shed their skins instead of growing old and dying. The entire universe was plastic, fluid, and inexhaustible. Crops grew spontaneously, and the flesh was replaced on animals soon after it was cut off.

CREATION OF THE COSMOS

Finally, the ancestors imposed an appearance upon the world, which has not changed much since that time, and enacted laws that are still in force. They created man out of earth or by transforming pre-existing indeterminate creatures or half-animals. At the same time, they created or formed the various species of animals and plants. In fashioning a single individual, they arranged for his descendants to resemble him so that all would benefit from the mutation of the archetype with no further intervention necessary. They also established the sea, dry land, islands, and mountains. They separated the tribes and instituted civilization, ceremonies, ceremonial details, rites, customs, and laws for each.

But by the fact that they contained each thing and each being within given limits, *natural* limits from that point on, they deprived them of all the magic powers that would permit them to gratify their wishes instantly and to become immediately anything they pleased, without encountering any obstacle. Order is, in fact, incompatible with the simultaneous existence of all possibilities, with absence of all rules. The world thus learns the unbreakable bonds that confine each species to its own being and prevent its escape. Everything became immobilized, and taboos were established in order that the new organization and legality should not be disturbed.

Lastly, death was introduced into the world by the disobedience of the first man, more frequently by the first woman, by the error of the "trickster"[25] ancestor, who, very commonly, clumsily tries to imitate the gestures of the Creator and whose imbecilic obstinacy leads to both comic and catastrophic consequences. In every way, with death as a worm in the fruit, the *cosmos* emerges from *chaos*. The era of chaos is closed, natural history begins, the rule of normal cause-and-effect is instituted. The burst of creative activity is succeeded by the vigilance necessary to maintain the universe that has been created in good order.

CHAOS AND GOLDEN AGE

It is evident that the mythical time seems clothed in a basic ambiguity. Indeed, it is described as having the antithetical quality of *chaos* and *golden age*. The absence of a dividing line attracts, as much as it repels, disorder and instability. Man looks nostalgically toward a world in which all he has to do to pick luscious and ever-ripe fruits is merely to reach out his hand; a world in which obliging crops are stored in his barn without working, planting, or harvesting; a world that does not know the hard necessity of labor; in which desires are realized as soon as conceived without becoming mutilated, reduced, or annihilated by a material obstacle or social taboo.

The golden age, the childhood of the world akin to the childhood of man, corresponds to this conception of an earthly paradise in which at first everything is provided, and upon leaving there man has to earn his bread by the sweat of his brow. It is the reign of Saturn and Cronus,[26] without war, commerce, slavery, or private property. But this world of light, tranquil pleasure, and easy, happy living is at the same time a world of darkness and horror. The time of Saturn is one of human sacrifice, and Cronus ate his children. The spontaneous fertility of the soil cannot be free of disaster. The first age is presented as the era of exuberant and disordered creation, of monstrous and excessive childbirths.

Soon, the two antagonistic conceptions become inextricably blended, then logically separated, then mythologically distinguished and opposed, chaos and golden age in succession. These seem like the two aspects of the same imaginary reality, that of a world without rules from which is derived the regulated world in which men now live. The opposition is like that of the world of myth to the world of history, which begins when the former ends. The contrast is even more like that of the world of dreams, as it is aptly called, to that of wakefulness. Lastly, it seems like a time of idleness, abandon, and prodigality, for the return of which man vainly hopes while seeing himself condemned to work, penury, and frugality.

At the same time, more or less obscurely, he doubtless thinks of his childhood. To establish it, there is no need of recalling the heartfelt regret and the trick of memory that cause the adult to embellish extremely the recollection of his youth, which now suddenly seems to have been devoted to play and exempt from care. He regards it as a time of eternal festivity in a garden of Eden. Moreover, he does not doubt that the two conceptions of the first age of the world and the *vert paradis des amours enfantines* shade into one another.

Also, it is a fact that, before the initiation ceremonies that introduce him into the social organization, the youth's activity is not governed by the taboos limiting the adult's behavior. For example, before marriage, in many cultures, the adolescent's sex life is generally the freest imaginable. It seems that then the individual is not yet part of the order of the universe, and as a result there is no risk of disturbing it by transgressing laws that do not concern him. He lives on the margins, so to speak, of the regulated universe, just as he lives on the border of organized society. Only half of him belongs to the cosmos, for he has not yet broken all his ties to the mythical universe, the beyond, where his ancestors have extracted his soul and caused it to be reborn in his mother's bosom.

In opposition to order and "natural history," the first age of the world represents a time of universal confusion that cannot be visualized without anxiety. Among the Eskimo, the contradictory aspects of the primordial era appear intimately intermingled. It has the characteristics of undifferentiated chaos. All was darkness, and there was no light on earth. Neither continents nor seas could be distinguished. Men and animals did not differ from one another. They spoke the same language, lived in similar houses, hunted in the same way. In the description of this epoch are also recognized the traits that usually portray the golden age. Talismans then had considerable power, for one could be transformed into an animal, plant, or pebble. The flesh of the caribou was replaced on its skeleton after it was eaten. Snow shovels moved about by themselves, so that they did not have to be carried.

But this last possibility already manifests, significantly, a mixture of regret and fear. It illustrates the desire for a world in which everything is achieved without effort, and causes fear of the shovels coming alive again and suddenly escaping from their owner. They can never be stuck into the snow, therefore, without being watched.

The Re-creation of the World

Simultaneously nightmare and paradise, the primordial age seems like the period or the state of creative vigor from which the present world escaped, with its vicissitudes of wear and tear and the threat of death. Consequently, it is by being reborn, by reinvigorating himself in this ever-present eternity, as in a fountain of youth with continuously running water, in which he has the chance to rejuvenate himself and to rediscover the plenitude and robustness of life, that the celebrant will be able to brave a new cycle of time.

This is the function fulfilled by the festival. It has already been defined as a re-enactment of the creative period. To use again Dumézil's apt formulation, it constitutes a passage to the great age, the moment when men stop their activity in order to gain access to the reservoir of all-powerful and ever elemental forces represented by the primordial age. It takes place in churches and shrines, which similarly are thought of as passages to the great void in which the divine ancestors evolved, and whose sites or consecrated mountain peaks are the visible landmarks associated with the decisive acts of the Creators.

Then one proceeds to the ceremony that is a critical phase of the seasonal cycle. It is then that nature seems to renew itself—when it visibly changes, as at the beginning or end of winter in arctic or temperate climates, and at the beginning or end of the rainy season in the tropical zone. With intense emotion, simultaneously reflecting anxiety and hope, a pilgrimage is made to the places that once were frequented by mythical ancestors. The Australian aborigines piously retrace their itinerary, stopping everywhere that they did and carefully repeating their actions.

Elkin has forcefully stressed this vital and religious bond, much more than merely geographic, that exists between the native and his country. The latter, he writes, appears to him as the pathway to the invisible world. It puts him in contact with "the powers that bestow life, to the advantage of man and nature." If he has to leave his native land or if it is over-run by colonization, he believes that he must die. He can no longer maintain contact with the sources of his periodic reinvigoration.

INCARNATION OF THE ANCESTOR-CREATORS

The festival is thus celebrated in the context of the myth and assumes the function of regenerating the real world. The time when vegetation renews itself and, the situation permitting, the place in which the totemic animal is abundant are chosen for this purpose. It is the place where the mythical ancestor created the living species from which the group is descended. The ritual of creation that has been handed down, and which alone is capable of leading to success, is repeated.

Actors imitate the heroic deeds and gestures. They wear masks that identify them with this ancestor, half-man and half-animal. Often these accessories are equipped with shutters that, at the desired moment, suddenly reveal a second face, thus allowing the wearer to reproduce the instantaneous transformations that took place in the first age. It is, in fact, important to conjure up the active presence of the beings from the creative period, who alone have the magic quality that can confer the desired efficacy upon the rite. Besides, no clear-cut distinction can be made between "the mythical base and the actual ceremony." Daryll Forde has explicitly shown this for the Yuma of Colorado. His informants continuously confused the rite that they were accustomed to celebrate with the act through which their ancestors instituted it originally.

Various procedures are employed concurrently to recreate the fecund time of the powerful ancestors. Sometimes the recital of the myths suffices. By definition, these are secret and powerful narratives that retell the creation of a species or the founding of an institution. They are as exciting as passwords. To recite then is sufficient to provoke the repetition of the act that they commemorate.

Another way of conjuring up the mythical period consists in retracing on rocks and in remote caves the paintings that represent their ancestors. In coloring and retouching them periodically (it must not be completely finished on one occa sion for continuity would be broken), the beings that they depict are recalled to life or *actualized,* so that they can assure the return of the rainy season, the multiplication of edible plants and animals, and the increase of spirit-children that make women pregnant and guarantee the prosperity of the tribe.

Sometimes a truly dramatic representation is encountered. In Australia, the Warramunga pantomime the life of the mythical ancestor of each clan, for example, for the people of the black snake, the life of the hero Thalaualla from the moment that he leaves the ground to the moment he returns. The actors have their skin covered with down, which falls off as they move. Thus they depict the dispersion of the seeds of life emitted from the ancestor's body. Having done this, they assure the multiplication of black snakes. Then men in their turn are restored, regenerated, and confirmed in their intimate being by consuming the sacred animal.

It has been seen that the latter is sacrilegious and taboo, when it is a question of respecting the order of the universe and not renewing it. But presently, the members of the clan are identified with the beings of the mythical epoch who do not know the taboos, and who instituted them when they came into being. During the preceding period, the officiants are, in effect, sanctified by a vigorous fast and many taboos, which cause them to pass gradually from the profane world to the domain of the sacred. They have become ancestors. The masks and ornaments that they wear are the sign of their metamorphosis. They can then kill and consume the animal, gather and eat the plant of which they mystically partake. Thus, they realize their communion with the principle from which they derive their power and their life. With it they absorb a new influx of vigor. Then they abandon to people of other clans the species that they happened to resurrect and deconsecrate, by making first use of this holy nourishment, identical with themselves, and that they need to taste periodically in an act of animating cannibalism, of strengthening theophagy. From this moment on, they will no longer eat freely of it. The festival is ended, and order is once again established.

FERTILITY AND INITIATION RITES

Fertility ceremonies are not the only ones. Others have as their goal to make youths enter the society of men and thus add them to the collectivity. These are initiation rites. They seem exactly comparable to the preceding rites and like them are founded on the representation of myths related to the origins of things and institutions.

The parallelism is absolute. Fertility ceremonies assure the rebirth of nature, and initiation ceremonies assure the rebirth of society. Whether they coincide or are celebrated separately, they consist equally of making the mythical part real and present, in order to make a rejuvenated world emerge.

In the *Madia*[27] cult of New Guinea, novices enter the sacred place acting as if newly born. They feign to be ignorant of everything, not to know the use of any utensil, to encounter for the first time the food they are given to eat. Then for their instruction, actors incarnating their divine ancestors present each thing in the order in which myths tell of its creation through their intervention. There is no good way of noting at what point the ceremony signifies the return to primordial chaos and, especially, the establishment of cosmic law. The coming of order into the world did not happen at one stroke, but was itself accomplished in orderly fashion.

According to Wirz, the *Madía* fertility and initiation ceremonies are identical. They only differ in their goals. In fact, society is always paired with nature. The novice is similar to the seeds in the ground, to soil that has not yet been cultivated. Their ancestors originally transformed monstrous creatures of the great age into men and completed them by giving them sexual organs, the sources of life and fertility. Initiation similarly makes true men out of the neophytes. Circumcision *perfects* their phalluses. The entire ceremony confers various virile qualities upon them, particularly bravery, invincibility, and in addition, the right and power of procreation. It leads the new generation of men to maturity, just as rites performed for the reproduction of the totemic species assure the growth of the new crop or the new animal generation.

After initiation, the novices learn the myths, the mysterious and sacred tribal heritage. They assist in performing ceremonies that they will celebrate in their turn, the success of which will prove the excellence of their adult qualities. The ritual dances of North America are tied to magic gifts, which are themselves related to the secret narratives that explain how their ancestors acquired them. Knowledge of the story and performance of the dance confer, for example, "possession" of the magic harpoon indispensable to the success of the otter hunt, of the brandy that revives the dead, and the burning fire that consumes from a distance. The dance is nothing else for the Kwakiutl, writes Boas, than "the dramatic representation of the myth related to the acquisition of the spirit," and as a consequence the gift that it personifies.

It has been revealed by the spirit itself to the novice who, in order to authenticate his initiation, repeats the dance while wearing the mask and emblems of the ancestor-protector who has taught it to him. In dancing, he incarnates it in animal form, for the ceremony was, as always, established in the mythical era before the Creator had fixed all things in their definitive forms. The spirits only appear in winter, that is, between two periods of profane labor, outside of ordinary times. Winter is the season for festivals, for dances in which youths incarnate spirits and by identifying with them acquire the gifts that they dispense and appropriate the powers they possess.

In mythical times, the two kinds of ceremonies (initiation and fertility) had become only one. Strehlow confirms this especially for Australia, where, moreover, they are most clearly distinguished in ritual. Ancestors frequent the great void with their novices and teach them, through performance, the rites by which they created beings or established them in a stable structure. Thus they initiated them, not by a "pale" ceremony, but by direct and effective demonstration, by the gift of their creative activity.

SUSPENSION OF THE RECORDING OF TIME

In every way, the primordial age must first be actualized. The festival is chaos rediscovered and newly created. In China, the leather bottle that symbolizes chaos is considered transformed when it has been pierced seven times by lightning. Again, man has seven apertures in his face, and a man who is well-born has seven in his heart. Outer chaos is symbolized by a stupid man, "without openings," without a face or eyes. At the end of a feast, lightning strikes seven times, not to kill, emphasizes Granet, but to cause rebirth and patterning to a higher existence. Shooting arrows into the leather bottle appears to be connected ritualistically with a winter festival, with drinking bouts all night long. This takes place during the last twelve days of the year.

This is a widely diffused custom. The festival recalls the time of creative license, preceding and engendering order, form, and taboo (the three notions are related and, together, are the opposite of chaos). This period has a fixed place in the calendar. In fact, when months are counted by the time between new moons and a year by the earth's rotation about the sun, twelve days remain in suspense at the end of the solar cycle. They permit the two ways of measuring time to coincide. These interpolated days do not belong to any month or year. They are outside recorded time and simultaneously, seem designated for the periodic return and recreation of the great age.

These days are the exact equivalent of the entire year, its "replica," as expressed in the Rig-Veda with regard to the sacred days of mid-winter in Ancient India. Each day corresponds to a month, and what happens in the first foreshadows what will happen in the second. Their names are identical and in the same sequence. If they are counted in two-and-a-half year cycles as in the Celtic calendar of Coligni,[28] the interpolated period comprises thirty days, equivalent to a twelve-month sequence repeated two-and-a-half times.

THE PRESENCE OF GHOSTS

Whatever its duration, time is confused in both the beyond and this world. Ancestors or Gods, incarnated by the masked dancers, mingle with men and violently interrupt the course of natural history. They are present at the Australian totemic festivals, the New Caledonian *pilou,* and the Papuan and North American initiation ceremonies.

In addition, the dead leave their abode and invade the world of the living. All barriers are broken and nothing any longer prevents the trespassers from visiting their descendants during this suspension of universal order that the change from old to new year connotes. In Thailand, an infernal being opens the doors of the abyss and the dead emerge into the sunlight for three days. A temporary king governs the country, with all the prerogatives of a true sovereign, while the people are given to games of chance (a typical activity involving risk and waste, directly opposed to the slow and sure accumulation of wealth through work). Among the Eskimo, at the time of the winter festivals, the spirits are reincarnated in the members of the group, thus affirming its solidarity and the continuity of the generations. Then they are solemnly dismissed so that the normal conditions of life can resume their course.

When the festival season is parcelled out and distributed over the entire year, a period is always observed in which the dead are permitted to be diffused into the society of the living.

At the end of the time allotted for their annual invasion, they are sent back to their own domain by explicit entreaties. In Rome, on fixed dates, the stone that closes the *mundus* is raised. This is a hole in the palatine hill that is regarded as the passage to the infernal world, as a contraction of this world, and, as its name indicates, as the exact counterpart of the world of the living, to which it is symmetrical. It represents the epitome of the great void in contrast to the area of the profane and enables them to communicate. The souls wander at large in the city for three days in May, after which each family head chases them out of his house by spitting out berries that redeem him and his family from the incursion until the following year. The return of the dead is often linked to times of change. In all Europe, it is mainly during Saint Sylvester's Eve, that is, during the last night of the year, that ghosts, specters, and phantoms are permitted to be rampant among the living.

The Function of Debauchery

This interlude of general confusion that the festival connotes appears to be a time in which the order of the universe is suspended. That is why excesses are then permitted. It is a matter of contradicting the rules. Everything is done in reverse. In the mythical epoch, the course of time was reversed. One was born an old man and died a child. Two reasons coincide in these circumstances to make debauchery and extravagance appropriate. To be more certain of recapitulating the conditions of existence in the mythical past, one tries to do the opposite of what is customarily done. Also, all exuberance signifies an increase in strength that can bring nothing but abundance and prosperity in the coming spring.

Either reason leads to the violation of taboos and immoderate behavior, in order to profit by the suspension of the cosmic order so that the forbidden act may be performed, and so that the order may be permissibly and unrestrainedly abused. Also, all the prescriptions that protect the natural and social welfare are systematically violated. However, these transgressions still are deemed sacrilegious. They are an attack upon the traditional rules that on the morrow will become holiest and most inviolate. They truly involve major sacrilege.

In a general way, every circumstance in which the existence of society and the universe seems to be threatened and to require renewal through the influx of youthful and excessive vigor is part of the incentive to change. Under these conditions, it is not astonishing that license is resorted to that is analogous or identical to that of the interpolated day. This was to compensate for the effects of a plague, as reported for one Australian tribe at a time of epidemics. Another tribe regarded the aurora australis as a celestial fire threatening to consume them. On that occasion, the elders ordered wives to be exchanged.

It cannot be doubted how strongly the natives feel about restoring the universe that has been attacked in its very essence, when it is observed that the Fijians, whenever there is a crop failure and starvation is feared, have a ceremony called "creation of the earth." In fact, this demonstrates the exhaustion of the soil. It is celebrated in order to rejuvenate, to bring rebirth, to conjure away the ruin that lies in wait for men and the world.

SOCIAL SACRILEGES UPON A KING'S DEATH

When the life of society and nature is symbolized by the sacred person of a king, the hour of his death determines the critical moment that unleashes ritual license. This assumes a character corresponding strictly to the catastrophe that has occurred. The sacrilege is against social order. It is perpetrated at the expense of majesty, hierarchy, and power. There is no case confirming that the unleashing of long-repressed passions is due to the forced weakness of government or the temporary absence of authority. (The latter has never in the least resisted popular frenzy.) It is considered just as necessary as was obedience to the deceased monarch. In the Hawaiian Islands, the populace upon learning of the king's death commits every act ordinarily regarded as criminal. It burns, pillages, and kills, and the women are required to prostitute themselves publicly. On the Guinea Coast, reports Bosman, as soon as the people learn of the king's death, "each robs his neighbor, who in turn robs another," and these robberies continue until a successor is proclaimed. In the Fiji Islands, the facts are even clearer. The death of the chief is a signal for pillage, the subject tribes invade the capital and commit all types of brigandage and depradation. To avoid these acts, the king's demise was often kept secret, and when the tribes came to ask if the chief was dead, in the hope of devastating and sacking the community, they were told that his body was already decomposed. They then withdrew, disappointed but docile, for they had arrived too late.

This example shows that the time of license is exactly that in which the king's body decomposes, that is, of the period of acute infection and defilement that death represents. In this time of full and open virulence that is very potent and contagious, society must protect itself by showing its vitality. The danger ends only with the complete elimination of the putrescent substance of the royal cadaver, when nothing more is left of the remains but a hard, sound, and incorruptible skeleton. Then the dangerous phase is deemed to be over. The habitual pattern of things can be re-established. A new reign commences after this time of uncertainty and confusion during which the flesh of the guardian had melted away.

In fact, the king is a guardian whose role consists in keeping order, moderation and rules—principles that wear out, grow old, and die with him, that lose their power and efficacy at the same time as his physical strength decreases. Also, his death inaugurates a kind of interregnum of inverted efficacy, a rule of the principles of disorder and excess generating an effervescence out of which is born a new and reinvigorated order.

DIETARY AND SEXUAL SACRILEGE

In the same fashion, dietary and sexual sacrilege in totemic societies has as its goal to assure the group of subsist-ence and fertility for an additional period. License is tied to the ceremonies in which the sacred animal is renewed or in which youths are integrated into the society of men.

In fact, these rites inaugurate a new vital cycle and, consequently, play the precise role of the changing seasons in the more differentiated civilizations. Thus they constitute a return to chaos, a phase in which the existence of the universe and law is suddenly questioned. Taboos that ordinarily assure the proper functioning of institutions, the predictable progress of the universe, by separating the spheres of the permitted and the forbidden, are then violated. The revered species is killed and eaten by the group, and parallel to the great dietary crime, the great sexual crime is committed. The law of exogamy is violated.

Under cover of the dance and the night, and in defiance of kinship ties, men of the clan have sex relations with the wives of the complementary clan, who are originally from their clan and, therefore, are taboo. Among the Warramunga, the evening after the men of the Uluura moiety celebrate their initiation ceremony they lead their wives to the men of the Kingilli moiety, who, it is recalled, have made all the preparations for the Uluura festival. The latter have relations with the women who belong to their own moiety. Ordinarily, these incestuous unions cause a chill of terror and abomination, and the guilty are condemned to the most vigorous punishments. Yet in the course of the festival, they are permitted and obligatory.

It must be stressed that these sacrilegious acts are regarded as just as ritualistic and holy as the very taboos they violate. Like the taboos, they free man from the *sacred*. In the course of the *pilou*, the great New Caledonian festival, writes Leenhardt, a masked character arrives who contradicts all the rules. He does everything that is forbidden to others. Reincarnating the ancestor whose mask identifies him, he pantomimes and repeats the actions of his mythical patron who "pursues pregnant women and reverses emotional and social concepts."

MYTH AND INCEST

It is important to conform exactly to the legendary example of the divine ancestors who practiced incest. The original act of incest was most often between brother and sister.
That is the case for numerous Oceanic, African, and American tribes. In Egypt, Nut, the sky Goddess, each night comes
to have sexual relations with her brother Geb, the earth God.
In Greece, Cronus and Rhea are also brother and sister, and
if Deucalian and Pyrrha, who repopulate the world after a
flood, are not brother and sister, they are at least cousins, whom
the law of exogamy separates. More emphatically, incest is
characteristic of chaos. They are mutually inclusive. Chaos is
the time of mythical incest, and incest currently takes place
in order to loose cosmic catastrophies. Among the African
Ashanti, if the one who couples with a forbidden woman and
thus compromises the universal order has not received his
just punishment, hunters can no longer kill in the forests,
crops stop growing, women no longer give birth, and clans
intermingle and cease existing. "All is now chaos in the universe," clearly concludes the observer.

Among the Eskimo, sexual license clearly manifests a return to the mythical period. Orgies take place at the time of
the festival of the extinguishing of the lamps, which is celebrated at the winter solstice. All lamps are simultaneously
extinguished and later relit. Thus the changing year is recognized, localized, and honored. During the darkness symbolizing chaos, couples have sexual relations at the bottom of the
deep embankment that runs along the walls of the winter
house. All wives are then exchanged. Sometimes the principle
that determines these temporary unions is enacted. In Alaska
and Cumberland Sound, a masked actor who personifies the
Goddess Sedna matches men and women according to their
names, just as were their legendary ancestors after whom they
are named. Thus, the suspension of the ordinary rules of
sexual behavior signifies nothing else than a temporary ascent
to the beginning of the ancient time of creation.

Myths of incest are myths of creation. They generally ex-

plain the origin of the human race. The quality of the forbidden union and the characteristics of the dream-time are
added to the normal fertility of sexual union. Erotic practices
are particularly important among the Kiwai and Marind-
anim of Papua. They merely reproduce those practices that
enabled their ancestors to create edible plants. In the festival,
as Lévy-Bruhl has remarked, debauchery is equivalent to sym-
pathetic magic and to participation in the creative power of
the primordial beings.

THE VALUE OF SEXUAL LICENSE

The sexual act already inherently possesses a fecundating
power. It is *hot,* as the Thonga say, in that it generates a power
capable of increasing and exciting everything in nature that
manifests it. The orgy of virility occasioned by the festival thus
assists this function by the sole fact that it encourages and revives the cosmic forces. But this can result as well from any
other kind of excess or debauchery. Anything may play its role
in the festival.

Just as order, which preserves but is used up, is founded
on proportion and distinction, so disorder, which regenerates,
implies excess and confusion. In China, a continuous barrier
of taboos separates the sexes in all manifestations of public or
private life. Man and woman work separately in distinct occu-
pations. Moreover, nothing pertaining to one may come in contact with anything belonging to the other. But each time that
festivals are created, the joint action of both sexes is required
for sacrifices, ritual labor, and the casting of metals. "The collaboration of the sexes," writes Granet, "was as efficacious
when reserved for sacred moments, as it was sacrilegious at
normal times." The winter festivals ended in an orgy in which
men and women fought and tore off their clothing. Doubtless, this was not so much to strip themselves naked as to re-
clothe themselves in the clothing of victors.

In fact, the exchange of clothing seems like the very
mark of the state of chaos, as the symbol of the reversal of
values. It took place at the time of the Babylonian *Sacaea,*[29]

and among the Jews, at the orgiastic festival of *Purim*, in direct violation of the law of Moses. It is doubtless necessary to connect rites of this type with the dual disguise of Hercules and Omphale. In Greece in any case, the Argive festival in which boys and girls exchange clothing bears the significant name of *hybristika*. For *hybris* represents an attack upon the cosmic and social order, or disproportionate excess. The texts present it as a characteristic of the centaurs, monstrous half-men and half-animals of mythology, ravishers of women and eaters of raw meat, reincarnated, as Dumézil has recognized, in the masked members of initiation confraternities, violently intruding at the time of the new year, and like their legendary prototypes, typical violators of all the taboos.

EXCESSES IN FERTILITY RITES

Fertility is born of excess. To the sexual orgy, the festival adds the monstrous ingestion of food and drink. The "primitive" festivals, prepared long in advance, manifest to a high degree this character that is maintained in striking fashion in more advanced civilizations. At the Athenian Anthesteria, everyone is given a bottle of wine. Then ensues a kind of tournament, in which the victor is the one who is the first to empty his bottle. At Purim, the Talmud indicates that one must drink until it is impossible to distinguish the two cries specific to the festival, "May Haman be accursed" and "May Moredecai be blessed." In China, if the texts can be believed, food is stocked "in piles as high as hills," troughs are dug and filled with wine, on which boats could sail, just as a chariot race could be run across the accumulation of food.

Everyone must stuff himself with as much food as possible and become bloated like a distended leather bottle. The exaggeration of traditional descriptions manifests another aspect of ritual excess. This is the competition in boasting and bragging that accompanies the waste and sacrifice of accumulated wealth. The role of boasting duels in the festivals and drinking bouts of the Germans, Celts, and other peoples, is well known. The prosperity of the next harvest must be assured, by recklessly dispensing the contents of the granaries. In a sort of wager with destiny, ruinous consequences are courted in the attempt to be the one who will give away the most, so that destiny is obligated to return with compound interest what it has received.

Each one thinks that he will receive, concludes Granet in commenting on the Chinese data, "a better remuneration and a greater return for his future labor." The Eskimo reckons in the same way. These exchanges and the distribution of presents that accompany the festival of Sedna, or the return of spirits to the beyond, possess a mystic efficacy. They make the hunt successful. "Not by motives of generosity or chance, [but through reciprocity]" Mauss emphasizes, "gift exchange results in producing an abundance of wealth." What is still practiced in Europe, specifically on New Year's Day, seems like the meager vestige of an intense circulation of wealth, once destined to reinvigorate cosmic existence and restore the cohesion of social life. Economy, accumulation, and moderation define the rhythm of profane life, while prodigality and excess define the rhythm of the festival, of the periodic and exalting interlude of sacred life that intervenes and restores youth and health.

Similarly, the frenzied agitation of the celebration at which they are devoured is in contrast to the established routine of work that permits food supplies to be amassed. In fact, the festival not only involves debauches of eating, drinking, and sex, but also those of expression—words and gestures. Cries, ridicule, and insults, the give and take of crude pleasantries (obscene or sacrilegious) between the public and a procession that crosses through it (as on the second day of the Anthesteria, at the Lenaean rites, at the Great Mysteries, at the carnival, or at the medieval Festival of Fools), jesting tourneys between groups of women and men (as at the shrine of Demeter of Mysia near Pellana of Achaia) constitute the major verbal excesses.

Movements, such as erotic pantomime, violent gesticulations, and simulated and real conflict, do not lag behind. The obscene contortions of Baubo, by making Demeter laugh, reveal the nature of her lethargy, and make her fertile. One dances until exhausted and whirls about until dizzy. Atrocities are quickly provoked by the dance. At the fire ceremony of the Warramunga, twelve of the participants seize flaming torches. One, using his firebrand as a weapon, charges his opposite. Soon there is a general melee in which they strike and crack their heads with torches, and the bodies of the combatants are showered with burning sparks.

PARODY OF POWER AND SANCTITY

Forbidden and extravagant behavior does not seem to emphasize sufficiently the difference between the time of release and the time of control. Contrary acts are added to them. One tries to act in a way exactly the opposite of normal behavior. The inversion of all relationships seems manifest proof of the return to chaos, the epoch of fluidity and confusion.

Also, the festivals that endeavor to revive the primordial era, the Greek Cronia or the Roman Saturnalia, imply the reversal of the social order. Slaves eat at the master's table, ordering them about and mocking them, while the latter serve and obey them, submitting to their affronts and reprimands. In each house, a state in miniature is established. The high functions, the roles of priests and consuls, are confined to slaves, who then exercise a power that is ephemeral and a parody of real power. In Babylon, roles were equally reversed at the time of the Sacaean festival. In each family, a slave, dressed as a king, ruled over the household. An analogous phenomenon occurred with the hierarchy of the state. In Rome, a monarch was chosen for a day, issuing ridiculous orders to his subjects, such as to make the rounds of the house while carrying a flute-player on one's shoulders.

Certain data lead us to think that the false king met a tragic fate. Every debauchery and excess was allowed him, but he was put to death on the altar of the God-king, Saturn, whom he had reincarnated for thirty days. The king of chaos being dead, order was restored, and the regular government again directed an organized universe or a cosmos. On Rhodes, at the end of the Cronia, a prisoner was made drunk and sacrificed. At the Babylonian Sacaea, a slave was hung or sacrificed, who, during festival time, had fulfilled the king's role in the city, using the latter's concubines, giving orders in his place, affording the populace an occasion for orgies and luxury. Doubtless, it is necessary to bring together these false kings—doomed to death after having shown themselves, during the annual suspension of regular power, to be extreme tyrants, committing excesses and debauchery—with Nahusha (equally given to excess, outrage, and debauchery), who rules over the sky and earth during the retreat of Indra, "across forty-three yards of water" after the murder of Vritra. This is also related to Mithothyn, the usurping magician who governs the universe after the retreat of Odin, when the latter goes into exile in order to purify himself of the defilement contracted because of his wife, Frigga. More generally, one thinks of the temporary sovereigns, notably in Indo-European myths, who take the place of the true ruler of the Gods when he leaves to do penance for the sins with which he has been charged by the very exercise of his authority.

Everything suggests that the modern carnival be viewed as a sort of moribund echo of ancient festivals of the Saturnalian type. In fact, a cardboard effigy depicting an enormous king, colored and comical, is shot, burnt, or drowned at the end of the period of license. The rite no longer has religious validity, but the reason for it appears clear. As soon as an effigy is substituted for a human victim, the rite tends to lose its expiatory and fecundating value, its double aspect of liquidating past defilements and creating a new world. It takes on the character of parody, which is already implicit in the Roman festival and which plays an essential role in the medieval Festival of Fools or of the Holy Innocents.

The lower clergy celebrates the Festival of the Holy Innocents during the period of rejoicing that begins about Christmas-time. They proceed to elect a pope, a bishop, or a mock abbot, who occupies the throne until the Eve of Epiphany. These clerics wear feminine garb, intone obscene or grotesque refrains to the airs of liturgical chants, transform

the altar into a tavern table at which they feast, burn the remains of old shoes in the censer, and, in a word, devote themselves to every imaginable impropriety. Finally, an ass clad in
a rich chasuble is led into the church with great pomp, and
prayers are offered in its honor.

At the heart of these burlesqued and sacrilegious parodies,
the ancient preoccupation with the annual reversal of the
order of things is recognized. Perhaps it is even more evident
in the exchange of roles between nuns and school-girls in the
great convent of the Congregation of Notre-Dame, in Paris, on
Holy Innocents Day. The pupils are clothed in the nuns habits, and take charge of the class, while their teachers take their
place on the benches, and make believe that they are paying
attention. The same festival was celebrated at the Franciscan
Monastery of Antibes, where roles of priests and laity were
reversed. The clergy replaced the lay brothers in the kitchen
and garden, and the latter said Mass. They were clothed for
the occasion in sacerdotal vestments, ragged and turned inside
out. They read the holy books while holding them upside
down.

REGULATIONS AND INFRACTIONS

No doubt, in these latter-day manifestations, no more
should be seen than the automatic application in a new environment of a kind of atavism, a heritage of the times in
which it was felt vitally necessary to reverse everything or
commit excesses at the time of the new year. Only the principle behind the rite and the idea of temporarily substituting
the power of comedy for a regular power have been retained.

The festival represents a complex totality in other respects. It implies a farewell to time past, to the year that has
ended, and at the same time it implies the elimination of the
waste-material produced by the functioning of every economy
and the defilement associated with the exercise of all power.
In addition, one returns to the creative chaos, to the *rudis in-
digestaque moles,* from which the organized universe was born

and reborn. It inaugurates a period of license during the absence of the regular authorities.

At Tonkin, the great seal of justice is enclosed in a small box, symbolizing that the law is dormant. The courts are closed, and of all offenses, only murder is still recognized. But the punishment of those guilty of murder is postponed until the rule of law is restored. In the meantime, power is entrusted to a monarch charged with violating all taboos, and indulging in every excess. He personifies the mythical sovereign of the golden age of chaos. General debauchery rejuvenates the world, and strengthens the animating powers of nature that are threatened by death.

When it becomes necessary to re-establish order, to fashion the universe anew, the temporary king is dethroned, expelled and sacrificed. This eventually facilitiates his identification with the symbol of the primordial age, when it was reincarnated in a scape-goat, who was hunted or put to death. The spirits of the dead are again dismissed. The ancestral Gods leave the world of men. The dancers, who depicted them, bury their masks, and erase their pictures. Barriers between men and women are again erected, and sexual and dietary taboos are again in force.

The restoration achieved, the forces of excess necessary to reinvigoration must give way to the spirit of moderation and docility, to discretion which is the beginning of wisdom, and to everything that maintains and preserves. Frenzy is succeeded by work, and excess by respect. The sacred as regulation, as taboos, organizes creation, conquered by the sacred as infraction, and makes it endure. One governs the normal course of social life, the other governs its paroxysm.

EXPENDITURES AND PAROXYSMS

In fact, in its pure form, the festival must be defined as the paroxysm of society, purifying and renewing it simultaneously. The paroxysm is not only its climax from a religious, but also from an economic point of view. It is the occasion for the circulation of wealth, of the most important trading, of

prestige gained through the distribution of accumulated reserves. It seems to be a summation, manifesting the glory of
the collectivity, which imbues its very being. The group then
celebrates births to come, which assure its prosperity and future welfare. It takes to its bosom newly initiated members
upon whom its vigor is based. It takes leave of its dead and
solemnly affirms its loyalty to them. At the same time, it is the
occasion on which, in stratified societies, the different social
classes approach and fraternize with each other. And in societies, the different social classes approach and fraternize with
each other. And in societies with moieties, it is the occasion
for antagonistic groups to blend. They thus attest their solidarity, and cause the mystic principles incarnate in them,
which ordinarily are carefully segregated, to collaborate in
the work of creation.

"Our festivals," explains a Kanaka, "mark the movement
of the awl that is used to bind the parts of the thatched roof,
a single word for a single roof." Leenhardt does not hesitate
to comment on this declaration, "The summit of Kanaka society is not the head of the hierarchy, the chief, but rather the
pilou itself. It is the moment in which the allied clans, stimu-
lated by discussions and dances, together exalt the Gods,
totems, and invisible beings, who are the source of life, the
support of power, and the very condition of society."

In fact, when these exhausting and ruinous festivals are
abandoned, under the influence of colonization, society loses
its bonds and becomes divided. As varied as imaginable, all
taking place in a single season, or spread over the course of
the year, festivals everywhere still fulfil an analogous function.
They constitute an interruption in the obligation to work, a
release from the limitations and servitude of the human condition. It is the moment in which the myth or dream comes
alive. One exists in a time in which one's only obligation is
to spend and be spent in it. Acquisitive motives are no longer
admissible, for each one must squander and waste his wealth,
food, and sexual and muscular vigor in competition with
others. But it seems that in the course of their evolution, societies tend toward indifference, uniformity, equalization of

status, and relaxation of tensions. The complexity of the social organism, to the degree that it is admitted, is less tolerant of interruption of the ordinary course of life. Everything must continue today the same as yesterday, and tomorrow as today.

General turbulence is no longer possible. It no longer occurs at fixed times or on a vast scale. It is as if it were diluted in the calendar and necessarily absorbed in monotony and regularity. The festival is then succeeded by the vacation. To be sure, it is always a time of free activity, of interruption in the pattern of work, but it is a phase of relaxation, not paroxysm. The values are found to be completely reversed. In one case, each part is in its place, and in the other, everything is gathered at the same point. Vacations (as the very term indicates) appear as a void, or at least an easing of social activity. By the same token, they are powerless to satisfy the individual. They are deprived of all positive character. The happiness they bring is primarily due to freedom from the boredom of which they are a distraction, from the obligations of which one has been freed. To go on vacation is first of all to flee care, to enjoy a "well-earned" rest. In addition, one is isolated from the group, instead of entering into communion with it, at a time of exuberance and jollity. Also, unlike the festival, vacations constitute not the flow of collective life but its ebb.

It, therefore, must be asked what brew of similar potency liberates the instincts of the individual, repressed by the exigencies of organized living, and at the same time leads to a collective effervescence of comparable magnitude. It seems that, with the rise of firmly established states, more and more strictly regulated as their structure affirms, the traditional alternation of merry-making and work, of ecstasy and restraint, that periodically cause order to be reborn from chaos, wealth from prodigality, and stability from disorder, is replaced by an alternation of a very different order, that, in the modern world, alone represents something comparable. It is the alternation of peace and war, prosperity and the destruction of the fruits of prosperity, regulated tranquility and obligatory violence.[30]

Chapter V—THE SACRED: CONDITION

OF LIFE AND GATEWAY TO DEATH

SOCIETY AND NATURE ARE CONSIDERED TO REST ON THE MAIN-
tenance of a universal order, protected by multiple taboos that
assure the integration of institutions and the regularity of phenomena. Everything that seems to guarantee their well-being and
stability is regarded as holy, and everything that seems to
compromise them is regarded as sacrilegious. Intermixture
and excess, innovation and change are equally dreaded. They
seem to be wearing or ruinous elements. Various kinds of
rites tend to expiate them, that is, to restore the order that
they have disturbed and to admit them to this order, by neutralizing the dangerous force or virulence that is revealed
solely by their intrusion and by their eruption into a world
which seeks only to endure and be at peace. It is then that
the cohesive quality of the sacred is opposed to its quality of
dissolution. The first sustains the profane universe and causes
it to endure, and the second threatens and shakes it, but renews it, and saves it from a slow death.

Whatever makes for cohesion and security is nourished
by sacrifice, and conversely, whatever makes for an increase
of power or pleasure, and every manifestation of vitality, implies risk or *hazard*. One must not live in order not to die, must
not become if one does not wish to cease being. If it were
necessary to formulate abstractly the conception of the world
that the polarity of the sacred seems to suggest, its alternately
inhibiting and stimulating role, it would be necessary to de-

scribe the universe (and everything in it) as composed of resistance and effort. On the one hand, taboos protect the order of the universe and keep excesses in check. They counsel an attitude of humility and a salutory sentiment of dependency. On the other hand, the recognition of obstacles engenders the energy to crush them. Submission implies the possibility of arrogance and revolt, stability and movement. To the vain conservation of wealth and power is opposed their fertile consumption, which no doubt destroys them, but this assures their resurrection. *Si le grain ne meurt . . .*

INERTIA AND ENERGY

Mythology in one form or other frequently opposes these antithetical elements of the sacred, which seem to illustrate the temptations to passivity and activity, respectively. Such, for example, would appear to be the distinction made by the Kanakas between totems and Gods. The first are the regulators of life. Taboos are respected, and people submit themselves to a required discipline in order to satisfy them. For them, the good administration of public resources is required, as well as the perfect conservation of nature and society, and a proper perpetuation of vital powers. Consequently, totems belong to the maternal line. Their aged uncles watch over them, protect them against attack, and check the rash impulses and risky enterprises of their nephews. By these acts, they always affirm their value and share their prestige.

Conversely, the heroic or ancestral Gods symbolize for their nephews, smarting under the prudent tyranny of the maternal line, glorious models that stimulate their trust, and sanction their ambition. The mythical destiny of the Gods foreshadows the real destiny of the nephews, in magnified and exalted fashion. In a certain sense, totems are the guardians of the rules and regulations that the Gods set forth to violate. This interplay of defense and offense, of restrictions imposed by the totem and conquests for which the Gods set an example, pushes Kanaka society to the dangerous brinks of anarchy and death, of disordered but sterile movement, or the stagnation of immobility.

Mythical antagonism corresponds to sexual and social antagonism. "The Gods are reality for men," affirms a native, "and totems come from women." Leenhardt stresses this formula by showing how the giddiness of power, which seizes the young chiefs and leads them to make a good bargain for the rights and dignity of their maternal relatives, institutes a permanent conflict between the two poles of collective existence. These are reincarnated, respectively, in their aged uncles watching over the transmission of the living heritage, and their nephews consumed by lust for power and change. "The life part," he writes, "maintains the necessity for conformity to the rules of existence, and the power part opposes to this the advantages of force and wealth."

Such an antagonism of wisdom and audacity, of the desire for rest and the spirit of adventure, seems like the aspect of collective existence that is most obviously reflected in the way in which the individual interprets the sacred. In time, the conflict is mentally projected only in myths and stories and is given reality by an effective competition for supremacy. "The maternal uncle falls by the spear of his nephew," affirms a Molagasy proverb, which, properly reinterpreted, could not only refer to the rivalry between old men and youths, but also that of static and dynamic social organisms and the warfare between the elements that preserve and those that make for the expenditure of life.

Similarly, in Greek mythology, there has been recognized in the idea of *moira*—that is to say, in the notion of an impersonal, blind, and impartial law—the passive element of the sacred, with which the active element, represented by the strivings of heroes and Gods, is in conflict. Heroes and Gods can "rectify" destiny and can deviate from what is fated. In the *Iliad,* Zeus is depended upon to change the lot of his son Sarpedon whose last hour has approached, but the danger of such a transgression is so great that the God dare not take responsibility for it. By causing his personal caprice to prevail over cosmic law, he would set an example of disorder and rebellion and would create a deadly precedent that would permit every God, and then every mortal, similarly to satisfy his impulses and instinctive needs.

In contrast to the uniformity of the universal order, the Gods seem like principles of individuation. They have a personality. They establish a type. Youths identify themselves with a young God-like Apollo, maidens with a Goddess-like Artemis, and married women with one like Hera. Not only do age and sex grades have patron saints, but also castes, social classes, and occupational groups. Warriors have a divine sponsor in Indra, and blacksmiths have one in Hephaestus.

The order of the universe presupposes a barrier of inhibitions, and the example of the Gods or heroes encourages release from inhibitions. The one restrains action, the other provokes it. They reign in turn over society, one during the debilitating phase, or time of work, and the other during the phase of paroxysm, the festival (or war). The affirmations of excessive vitality, intoxication, violence, ecstasy, feasts and orgies, prodigality, and games of chance—severely repressed during the static period because they distract men's arms from collective labor and their minds from communal pursuits and the accumulation of wealth in the public interest—become, on the contrary, during periods of crisis, a means of exalting communion. The latter makes for a feeling of rejuvenation, a restoration of society. Consequently, society is in fact restored and rejuvenated, because in these matters, sentiment precedes and engenders fact.

INTERNALIZATION OF THE SACRED

With the rise of civilization, with the beginning of the division of labor, still more with the rise of the city and the state, festivals lose importance. They symbolize less and less the magnitude and total character that made the ancient effervescences a complete suspension of institutional interaction and a basic challenge to the universal order. A more complex society does not tolerate such a break in the continuity of its functioning. It insists upon the gradual abandonment of the alternation between phases of debility and paroxysm, of dispersion and concentration, of regulated and unrestrained activity, which is the rhythm of development at a time when collective life is less differentiated. Individual labor can be interrupted, but public services must not be stopped. General disorder is no longer admissible. At best, only a facsmile is tolerated.

Social life in its entirety tends toward uniformity. More and more, flood and draught are channelized into a regular and even flow. The multiple needs of profane life tolerate less and less the simultaneous reservation of the same time for the sacred by everyone. Also, the sacred becomes fragmented, becomes the specialty of a sect that leads a semi-clandestine existence, or in the majority of cases, becomes the concern of a specialized group that celebrates its rites in a remote place and remains in office for a long time. Sooner or later, its divorce from the state is consecrated by the separation of the spiritual from the temporal. Then the church no longer coincides with the city, and religious and national boundaries no longer are the same.

Religion soon becomes dependent upon man, no longer upon the collectivity. It becomes universalistic, but also, in correlative fashion, personalistic. It tends to isolate the individual by confronting him with a God that he then knows less through rites than through a diffusion of personalized intimacy. The sacred becomes internalized and no longer attracts only the mind. The importance of the mystical increases and that of the cult diminishes. Any external criterion seems inadequate, from the moment that the sacred becomes less an objective manifestation than a pure attitude of mind, less a ceremony than a profound sensation. It is with reason under these conditions that the word "sacred" is used outside the properly religious domain to designate that to which each devotes the better part of himself, that which is of utmost value and is venerated, that for which he sacrificed his life.

Such is, in fact, the decisive touchstone that permits the unbeliever to distinguish between the sacred and the profane. That being, object, or idea is sacred for which man departs from routine, that he does not allow to be discussed, scoffed at, or joked about, that which he would not deny or surrender at any price. For the lover, it is the woman he loves; for the artist or scholar, the work that he pursues; for the miser, the gold that he amasses; for the patriot, the welfare of the state, the security of the nation, and the defense of its territory; and for the revolutionist, the revolution.

It is absolutely impossible to distinguish these attitudes from those of the believer, except in the way they are applied. They demand the same self-denial, and they presuppose the same unconditional personal involvement, a similar asceticism and spirit of sacrifice. Without doubt, it is convenient to attribute different values to them, but that is an entirely separate problem. It is sufficient to note that they imply the recognition of a sacred element surrounded by fervor and devotion, of which one must avoid speaking, and which one must try to conceal, for fear of exposing it to some sacrilege (insult, ridicule, or merely a critical attitude) on the part of the indifferent, or one's enemies, who would not respect it.

The presence of such an element entails a certain number of sacrifices in the ordinary course of life, and, in the event of a crisis, the sacrifice of life itself is agreed to in advance. Everything else is considered profane, is used without excessive scruples, is evaluated, judged, doubted, and treated not as an end but as a means. Some subordinate everything to the preservation of life and property, and thus seem to regard everything as profane, taking the greatest liberties they can with them. Of course, self-interest or the pleasure of the moment governs them. For them alone, it is clear that the sacred exists in no other form.

THE CHOICE OF A SUPREME END

On the contrary, those who rule their conduct by complete devotion to some principle tend to re-establish about them a kind of sacred environment, which excites violent emotions of a special kind that are capable of assuming a characteristically religious, ecstatic, fanatical, or mystical quality.

On the social level, these emotions give rise directly or indirectly to dogmas and ritual, to mythology and worship. If contemporary examples must be cited, it would be sufficient to point out as a type of secular liturgy, the ceremony of the eternal light at the tomb of the Unknown Soldier under the Arc de Triomphe, and as a model of secular mysticism, the characteristic attitudes of party militants, which demand unqualified obedience of their members.

In a general way, the different values that elicit total dedication and that are basic to every issue have their partisans and martyrs, who serve as models for the believers. Real or legendary, most often drawn from history and exemplifying rather than engendering a mystical theme, they furnish precept and example. Stories of their lives and deaths inspire everyone and impel one to identify with them privately and, if need arises, to imitate them.

It is impossible either to trace the major trends in the history of the sacred or to analyze the forms that it assumes in contemporary civilization. At best, it can be noted that it seems to become abstract, internalized, and subjective, attached less to beings than to concepts, less to acts than to intentions, and less to external manifestations than to spiritual tendencies. This evolution is manifestly tied to the most important phenomena in the history of humanity—such as the emancipation of the individual, the development of his intellectual and moral autonomy, and the final triumph of the scientific ideal. The latter is an attitude hostile to mystery, demanding systematic skepticism, a deliberate lack of respect. In considering everything as an object of knowledge or a matter of experience, it leads to everything being regarded as profane, and consequently viewed as knowable, with the possible exception of the passion for knowledge itself.

In addition, it is certain that these new conditions of the sacred have led to its assuming new forms. Thus, it invades ethics and transforms such concepts as honesty, fidelity, justice, and respect for truth and promises, into absolutes. Basically, everything happens as if it sufficed to make an object, being, or cause sacred, that it be dedicated and consecrated to a supreme end. One's time, energy, interests, and ambitions are devoted and sacrificed to its demands. One publicly attributes great prestige to it and shows that he renounces the most commonly esteemed goods in its favor, those most greedily pursued and conserved. In this situation, the dichotomy of sacred and profane no longer seems bound to the concept of the order of the universe, to the rhythm of its aging and regeneration, and to the opposition between neutral or inert objects, energies that animate or destroy them, that inherently attract or repel.

It has not been able to resist the transformation of social life that has brought about the increasing independence of the individual, freeing him from every psychic constraint and protecting him from others. Moreover, the sacred persists to the degree that this liberation is incomplete, that is to say, whenever a value is imposed as a reason for being upon a community and even an individual. The sacred is now revealed as a source of power and contagion.

The sacred remains whatever stimulates respect, fear, and trust. It is imbued with power yet involves existence. It always appears as that which separates man from his fellow-men, removes him from vulgar preoccupations, makes him win out over the obstacles and dangers that most beset him. It introduces him into a harsh world. His instinct is to flee the sacred, even while attracted to it. In that world, the rule is no longer to preserve achieved status or to keep any status permanent. Stability is no longer regarded as the highest good, nor are moderation, prudence, or conformity to established usage regarded as among the highest virtues. Security, comfort, a good reputation, and honor are no longer deemed as most desirable advantages.

In fact, the profane attitude always implies a kind of abdication. It restrains man from the wanton gratification of his desires. It diverts him from using his mind wastefully, and places him on guard against perilous and ruinous instincts that incite him to countless expenditures. At the same time, it surrounds such insatiable heroes as Faust or Don Juan— who dared to assume these decisive risks, braving the infernal powers, or entering into a pact with them—with a halo of prestige.

These mythical figures, exemplars of destiny, live in the imagination as concrete symbols of the kind of grandeur and perdition reserved for those who violate taboos and are immoderate in feeling, intelligence, and desire. These damned ones have been lost by their very intrepidity. Theirs is the glory of not having accepted any divine or human limitation when it was a question of satisfying one of the unquenchable appetites of feeling, knowing, and dominating. These were condemned by Saint Paul, who referred to them as *libido sentiendi, libido sciendi,* and *libido dominandi.*

To these three lusts, there are no comparably opposing taboos. The latter are only an obstacle, a kind of challenge that exists only as a function of the courage that sets it off. What makes these ambitions their true and worthy counterpart are the inverted ambitions, such as the renunciation of sanctity, the joyous acceptance of chastity, ignorance, and obedience, the desire to feel nothing, to have nothing, to acquire nothing, even to desire nothing, and the taste for giving in place of the taste for taking. Thus, everywhere in the profane environment of conservation and economy, outside of every rite and every external manifestation, the fundamental ambiguity of the sacred is rediscovered. The dreaded world of sacrilegious conquests and the blessed world of sanctifying abandon are both consecrated by an equal disdain for the common condition, by a similar basic dissatisfaction, to which beatitude or damnation alone can put an end.

TIME AND DESTINY

Without doubt, it is out of place to outline the metaphysics of the sacred in ending this work, but at least, it can be indicated at what point the antagonism of the sacred and the profane is identified with the cosmic interaction that, in order to form future or past, to give life to being, comprises stability and variation, inertia and movement, mass and force, matter and energy. The nature of these oppositions involves more than their content. The relationships of solidarity and collaboration that they establish between the terms they simultaneously dissociate and associate are more significant than the way in which they are or are not conceived. Through the diversity of appearances, the continuity of the universe seems to result from the combination of the poles of obstacle and effort that can never be perfectly isolated. It is impossible to last without wear and tear or loss, and impossible to become motionless. To be so, it would be necessary not to live but to be as the "sleepers" in stories, deep in a magic sleep during which others grow old and are transformed, but from which they awaken, identically as they were, to a world they no longer recognize. They are no longer part of a world of metamorphosis, simple expenditures, and total activity. This can not occur without lassitude, scars, or nostalgia for annihilation, this taste of fatigue and death that victory and the exaltation of triumph convey

It would not be difficult to find, in the organic, and even the inorganic world, this solidarity of death and life, of the resistance seeking to paralyze all effort and the effort seeking to annihilate all resistance. However, it becomes exhausted by its very success, by the fact that in evolving action it also develops a force that checks it. The laws of biology, chemistry, and physics offer as many examples as desired of this mechanism on all levels of existence. Under these conditions, it is remarkable that it can be utilized as a key for the comprehension of the principal problems concerning the statics and dynamics of the sacred that have been formulated and examined in the course of this work.

The profane must be defined as the constant search for a balanced or just environment that permits living in fear and moderation without exceeding the limits of the allowable. One is content with a gilded mediocrity, which manifests the precarious collaboration of the two antithetical forces that assure the perpetuation of the universe through reciprocally neutralizing each other. The departure from this tranquillity, from this place of relative calm in which stability and security are greater than elsewhere, is equivalent to the entrance of the sacred into the world. Then man is abandoned to the pursuit of the only tyrannical component that in all life calls for concerted action. That is to say, he has now already consented to its loss as he takes the divine path of renunciation or the magical path of conquest, as he wishes to be saint or sorcerer, and as he unreservedly devotes himself to these activities.

In seeking for the principles of life, the energies of the *sacred*, which sustains and interferes with him, the being (object, organism, mind, or society) approaches it yet remains at a distance. The pages in which Saint Theresa of Avila describes her ecstasy must be read, in this regard. If one is careful to ignore the expressions that are too parochially Christian, it will be seen how the confidences of the saint illustrate this paradox, how contact with the sacred inaugurates a sorrowful conflict between the intoxicating hope of definitely falling into a deep abyss and the kind of sluggishness with which the profane weighs down every movement toward the sacred. Saint Theresa herself attributes this to the instinct for self-preservation. Returning the being that dies to life, so that it should not die, this sluggishness seems like the exact counterpart of the ascendancy exercised by the sacred upon the profane. It always tries, for its part, to renounce time in favor of a leap to ephemeral and extravagant glory.

The sacred is what gives life and takes it away, it is the source from which it flows, and the estuary in which it is lost. But the sacred is also that which one would not know how to possess simultaneously with life. Life is wear and tear, and waste. It vainly strives to persevere and to refuse every expenditure so as to be preserved. Death lies in wait for it.

There is no artifice that is as good. Everything living being knows or senses it. It knows the choice remaining to it. It dreads giving of itself, *sacrificing* itself, and is aware of thus wasting its very being. But to retain its gifts, energies, and resources, to use them prudently for all practical and selfish goals—as a consequence, profane—saves no one in the final analysis from decrepitude and the tomb. Everything that is not consumed rots away. Furthermore, the abiding truth of the sacred resides simultaneously in the fascination of flame and the horror of putrefaction.

Appendix I—SEX AND THE SACRED: SEXUAL PURIFICATION RITES AMONG THE THONGA

THE GOAL OF THIS STUDY IS TO SHED LIGHT ON THE PRINcipal characteristics of the sacred, in purely descriptive and concrete fashion, through the analysis of a complex of specific rites in a particular civilization. I have tried to note the originality of their underlying conceptions. Parenthetically, the sacred will be recognized as efficacious, indivisible, contagious, fleeting, ambiguous, and virulent, just as it has been defined by numerous writers, among whom must at least be cited Durkheim, Jevons, Robertson Smith, Söderblom, Hertz, and Preuss. Thus, this work has no other aim than to show, in a particularly clear-cut and well-studied instance, how the religious consciousness conceives the vehicle of these different qualities, and the beneficent or terrible manner in which they are manifested.

For this purpose, I have chosen the purificatory rites of a Bantu tribe, the Thonga. Not only are these rites known with a precision leaving nothing to be desired, but the entire daily existence of the Thonga, public and private, has been described in an exceptionally thorough fashion. There is no risk of misconstruing the meaning or implication of their actions, since it is impossible to replace them in the whole from which they have been extracted, and outside of which they often have little significance. Finally, the vocabulary used by the Thonga to account for their customs seems to express very conscious and, therefore, very understandable images and symbols, in their strangest and most unexpected aspects. The conjunction of these rare advantages perhaps justifies the present choice of this Bantu people for a study that will be of value, in addition, only when it is compared to parallel inquiries involving the greatest number of possible cases.[31]

Again, sexual rites are involved. For the sentiment of the sacred is always particularly striking and in high relief with regard to everything that touches upon sexuality. It is noteworthy that the Freudian school has boldly and systemically, as is its practice, believed it possible to identify the sexual with the sacred and even to derive the sentiment of the sacred from the fear of sex. That is working too quickly. In fact, to explain the behavior of "primitives,". it is scarcely reasonable to resort to anxiety complexes, traumatic experiences, and repressions of which they generally have no knowledge. For the most part, until marriage they regard sex play as free, natural, and of no consequence. The idea cannot be escaped that these enthusiastic scholars, assured as they are of the validity of their solution for every problem, have too quickly projected the complexes of the "civilized" upon "savages."

If sexuality and the sacred readily coincide, it is entirely for other reasons. First, the polarity of the sexes furnishes sometimes the model and sometimes the basis for the dichotomizing of nature and society into complementary and antagonistic principles that, in justifying taboos and directing exchanges, are at the heart of "the sacred as respect." Second, since sex determines reproduction, it is inevitable that it be associated with the rites of fertility and, successively, puberty and initiation. The latter, in order to validly admit boys and girls to the dynamic and responsible collectivity, transform them through a final modification of their bodies into complete and potent adults capable of fighting and procreation. In the third place, the sexual organs and secretions furnish, through the magic of apertures and temperament, abundant occasions for the development of the most varied beliefs and practices. Finally, the blood from menstruation, defloration, and childbirth is a powerful contributing factor in the regarding of the female, as simultaneously weak, wounded, impure, and evil. She naturally belongs to the sacred "left," and her presence or contact on certain occasions must be feared. Numerous religious prescriptions relative to purity and defilement have no other origin.

For these many reasons, it was profitable to choose a complex of rites in which sexuality plays a fundamental role in order to clarify the characteristics of the sacred. It could legitimately be hoped that there they would be clearer, more coherent, and more significant than in most cases.

Upon the death of an individual, the Thonga consider that the defilement of his death reaches, above all in his relatives, to the source of life. It strikes at the seminal fluid of the men and the vaginal secretions of the women. During mourning, and from the first pangs of death, all sex relations are forbidden to the inhabitants of the village. Purification is necessary in order to lift the taboos that weigh on everything that has been contaminated by the deceased—food, gardens, inheritances, relatives, and grave-diggers. Presently, the great rite of liberation is precisely the sexual act itself. The ceremony is called *hlamba ndjaka*, literally, "purification of the objects of the dead." In fact, the word *ndjaka* has two meanings, and those who inherit the property of the deceased are called "eaters of *ndjaka*."

On the day fixed for the rite, men and women are grouped apart from each other. An inquiry is then launched on how well the ritual taboo has been observed. (I, 147). If someone has violated it, he must begin the rite, otherwise the leader of mourning, the next of kin of the deceased, begins. Thus, by all means, the dangerous honor of inaugurating the lustral rite is reserved for the most defiled. He and his wife retire to the brush and have sexual intercourse, but he must be careful to withdraw before ejaculating. The woman then takes in her hands their two "defilements," his sperm and her vaginal secretions, and anoints their navels with it. They return to the village by detours, and the woman goes to wash her polluted hands. All the couples act the same. Each woman cleans her hands in the same place, which is then trampled by the men. The clothing belonging to those absent and to very young children is equally purified, since the latter are not considered strong enough to assist in the ceremony without dying. (In reality, they are incapable of performing the ritual.) It is a matter of ridding the entire village of the impurity that undermines it. Lastly, men and women bathe in a river, men upstream and women downstream (I, 148), doubtless because the latter are considered more impure. They have nothing to fear from the less dreaded defilement that the water brings and will carry away together with theirs.[32]

The meaning of the rite seems clear. The men and women of the village are contaminated by the dead at the very source of their being. As a consequence, they must rid themselves of the defilement without its infecting whatever may be exposed to it. That is why the sexual union takes place in the brush, and why the semen is discharged outside the female. This external emission of the contaminated fluid exactly constitutes purification. The proof of this is that if someone, through impotence or due to old age, is unable to ejaculate, the others continuously ask him, with anxiety, if he has succeeded. If he is unable, the whole ceremony is interrupted. It becomes inauspicious to finish the rite, and the impotent one must submit to a harsh fast, designed to make him recover the power to expel his defilement.

Those who have accomplished the rite anoint their navels with the fluids that have been emitted. They thus profit by their potency and make use of the fluid's energy, but they are careful to eliminate all other residues. This involves the women washing their hands which have touched and collected the contaminated secretions; the trampling of the place where the washing took place and the water was spilt (the defilement must be thrust deep into the ground); and the final bath in running water by the men and the women. One understands the name that the Thonga give to the ceremony, *lahla khombo,* that is to say, "expulsion of bad luck." They also say that it "cures mourning," this focus of infection that resides in the sources of individual life (I, 149).

The purificatory ritual that is used in the event of sexual intercourse between husband and wife prior to the expulsion of the bad luck and the cure of mourning comprises equivalent and no less typical practices, arranged in analogous order. The male is at first subjected to a strict diet, without which he would swallow the "contamination of the dead" and the village would have to be again entirely purified. Then the female wipes the sexual parts of her husband, as well as her own, with one of her undergarments, the dirtiest possible, that she afterwards burns. Then they warm their heads and hands in the flames, and the woman gathers the ashes, mixes them with grease, and anoints her husband's private parts with this mixture. Then they sleep together for two consecutive nights, without it being known whether the sex act is completed or the seminal fluid is spilt outside. A sequence is observed that is already well-known. The defilement is gathered together, destroyed by fire (instead of being eliminated in running water), exposed to the purifying flames, and anointed with ashes as a remedy appropriate to the evil. Finally, purification is achieved (if *coitus interruptus* is practiced) or normal conjugal relations are restored, and the reinvigorating quality of the sexual act is utilized (if the sex act is completed).

Still more significant is the purification ritual for widows. They are organized for initiation into a kind of secret society. Several days after the reunion that determines their provisional redistribution among the relatives of the deceased, the men of the village send them, each with a friend as a witness, into the neighboring areas, and say to them: "Go and disperse the malediction through the countryside, before another evil befalls you." That is because the defilement or malediction is due to and attracts bad luck. Caused by misfortune, it is nothing but an occasion for trouble, weakness, and more misfortune. It is urgent that it be eliminated. Thus the widows leave, and under the pretext of visiting a relative enter a kraal and try to seduce a male. But, having reached their goal, they try to escape the mixing of semen during the sex act in order to leave the defilement in the man. The one who succeeds returns joyfully proclaiming, "I have fought against mourning, and conquered it." But the man seeing the woman disrobing knows that she is a widow and that she wants to "kill" him. Therefore, he calls his friends to the rescue, to hold her motionless until he ejaculates. In this case, he remains pure and she is defiled. She has been "conquered by mourning," and abandons herself to shame and despair (I, 484).

It is not hard to understand the reasons for this behavior. The defilement of the dead, this active force of destruction that must be conquered, is particularly present in the sexual secretions of the widow. If she succeeds in *passing* it to the man, and impregnating his sex organ with these secretions, without allowing him to leave his sperm in her, she is rid of it. If the man, on the contrary, withdraws after his seminal emission, he leaves the defilement with her and ejects what his sex organ has contracted by contact with the contaminated mucus of the widow.

Despite the strangeness of the comparison, everything takes place just as in the game of tag. The one who is "it" *passes* on his quality by touching a player on the hand, but he must avoid being touched in turn by the latter, for he would then become "it" again. The man who succeeds in emitting his semen into the widow is exactly comparable to the child who, instead of fleeing the player who is "it," resolutely waits for him, and by touching him immediately after he has been touched, immediately places upon him the especially contagious and dangerous quality involved in being "it." This is comparable in many respects to the state of defilement. In order to avoid this maneuver, the children frequently agree that it is not permitted to retouch one's *father*, a word that is extremely significant. Outside of play, this rule is injurious. Rites are performed not to assure, but to eliminate the circulation of impurity. Therefore it is always permissible to lead the impurity back to its source, *to touch one's father again*.

The man who did not see until too late that he was involved with a widow must, in his turn, rid himself of the defilement of the dead that has been passed to him. He then has recourse to the medicine-man. Sometimes, being suspicious, he takes the precaution before the sex act of tearing a piece off the undergarment of the woman who made advances to him. Later, he asks the medicine-man to concoct a potion for him in which this piece of material is one of the ingredients. Then he wraps himself in a blanket, burns the magic compound over the flaming embers, and inhales the smoke. He thus escapes the danger of dying (I, 293).

It should be noted that an identical procedure is employed by the man who is defiled by intercourse with a woman, before she has been purified (by passing through water) of every trace of menstrual blood. Drinking a potion, analogously concocted, saves his life. Without this, his sex organs would enter his body and he would die through no longer being able to urinate or expel his impurities (I, 483). In this case too, a piece of material must be borrowed from the undergarment of an indisposed female. This, too, is accounted for by virtue of the principle *similia similibus curantur*. The clothing of an indisposed woman cures the defilement due to menstrual blood, just as a widow's cures the defilement of death.

The widows who have succeeded in "conquering mourning" arrange to come back together to the village.[33] At the main entrance, they emit ritualistic cries. Everyone comes out to meet them, and they are solemnly conducted to the tomb of the deceased. They inform him that have left the pariah state in which death has placed them. This is a day of rejoicing for the village.

Then there is nothing left but to complete purification that will return them to the profane and free world. First, the widows change their undergarments in which some defilement may persist and take a steam bath. That evening, each is permitted to receive in her hut the man to whom she has been provisionally assigned, and who has made regular visits there. It is necessary that they "kill the mourning." To this end, they shut themselves in the hut, drink purificatory medicines, place pills on the fire, and expose their sex organs to the smoke. After this, they extinguish the fire with their urine, and have intercourse as many times as they are able, the male always withdrawing before ejaculating—in order to prevent children, indicates the native informant (I, 194, 484). Without doubt, no good can come of conceiving at a time of impurity, but it is also true, and perhaps more important, that the widow's purification be completed (there is no such thing as too many precautions). Now that most of the defilement's infectiousness has been transmitted to a stranger, it is the role of the future husband to finish the work that has been started, that is, to finish *conquering* and *killing* mourning, to finish in both senses of the word, after having been immunized by medications against the contagion of the last traces of defilement.

It does not occur to them to ask, as does Junod, why the sexual act, regarded as dangerous under many circumstances in life, here assumes the supreme purificatory role. The interrupted sex act, having lustral value, is not, properly speaking, a sexual act. It does not have a *savage, ferocious,* or *passionate* character, to use Junod's very words. For it is thanks to this characteristic that the sex act is regarded as stimulating and exacerbating the powers of good and evil that are diffused throughout nature.[34] Also, when the contamination of the deceased rages through the village at the death of one of its inhabitants, and for a stronger reason at times of epidemics, sex relations are strictly taboo. They would increase the infection that it is important to "conquer." That is why married men must not approach the newly circumcized. They would prevent the healing of the wound. They must not enter the hut of a sick man, for they would stimulate the virulence of the malady. They must not have sexual intercourse during the time of hunting or fishing, for the fish or game would become too lively or vigorous. Conversely, a little boy and a little girl lie on a lionskin beside a lake, just as if they were husband and wife, but ordered to be quiet in the hope that the fish will remain motionless and allow themselves to be easily caught.

A couple of children play the same role of invitation at the time that a big fire is made ready, for example. Their rest will prevent the flame from becoming too great. For the same reason, the potter's kiln is not to be lit by a married woman (I, 178–79; II, 313, *fn* 1 and 314). The reason suggested by the natives is perfectly clear. Married people are *hot*. They therefore communicate their *heat,* the vital power emanating from sex relations, to whatever they approach. Also, they must stay at a distance from everything that it is important to appease, calm, or weaken, such as illness, game, defilement, and the contagion of death. On the other hand, for stimulating the fertility of the soil, sexual intercourse is utilized.[35]

It is known that the sex act is generally regarded as beneficial for agrarian rites. An immediate sacred union three times in succession has no other function. At the time of the *hlamba ndjaka* itself, sex relations are engaged in as a stimulant. When the woman, with whom the widower is purified, goes to bring the lustral water to her relatives in their village, her husband accompanies her, if the journey is long, and has intercourse with her on the eve of their arrival in order to renew the quality of the liquid (I, 149). Again, the sex act is vitally required at the founding of a new village (I, 178).

The indisposed woman is *hot* in the same way. Her purification makes her *cold* again. The word used, according to Junod, compares her to a pot removed from the fire (I, 483). What a taboo corresponds to, the exact nature of a defilement, and how its dual aspect of active force and infectious energy is explained can hardly be made clearer. It is a heat capable of burning and consuming, but also, when properly appeased and controlled, of cooking and of the acceleration of life. In any case, the being or thing that it imbues cannot be approached without care, like the pot containing succulent viands which is too hot and, therefore, cannot be touched until it has reached a temperature at which it can be grasped without danger. Conversely, the nursing mother who, because of absence, has not given her breast to her infant for more than one day, must reheat her milk. She squeezes a few drops of it onto a hot potsherd. Without doing this, the cold milk would constipate the child. Cold slows and paralyzes, and heat stimulates and excites.

Thus the sex act results in defilement to the degree that its frenzied aspect puts forces into play whose effects are impossible to control. The purificatory rite, of the *hlamba ndjaka,* on the contrary, does not imply any unbridling, but rather a certain self-control. It is not a question of hastening the secretion of the vital fluids of the man and the woman but rather, since the latter have become defiled by the contamination of the dead, of making them get rid of this infection of their organisms through a delicate operation that is difficult to conduct successfully and interrupt at the proper time.

The energy of these vital principles is easily confirmed in other circumstances. A woman in childbirth, defiled by the blood from parturition, submits to severe and numerous taboos that cut her off from the community. Medicines are administered to expel the impure blood that still contaminates her. Her husband, to stay pure, must not enter her hut. At the fall of the umbilical cord, the mother of the woman in childbirth spreads clay on the floor of the hut (just as the indisposed woman does at the end of her periods), so that the feet of those who have again been permitted to enter should not tread on it or be exposed to walking over any trace of noxious blood.

The return of menstruation to the young mother signifies the return of the normal and periodic evacuation of impurity. Also, from this moment on, the father can take the infant in his arms. He no longer risks defilement through embracing a being in permanent contact with a contaminated organism.

About one year later, when the child begins to crawl, the parents procure their respective sexual liquids by an incomplete sex act (just as in the case of eliminating the impurity of the deceased). The mother takes this "defilement" in her hands and spreads it on a cotton string that the child wears about its loins, which remains there until it wears away. Afterward, the child is a "big person." He has become such through the beneficent quality of the vital fluids of his parents. From this time on, if he dies, he is buried in holy (dry) ground instead of accursed (humid) ground with twins, premature babies, and those whose upper teeth came through first—in a word, with all rejected ones and monsters that until their last breath were kept isolated from the community of the pure by the group. In addition, the child now takes part in the purification of mourning (I, 59 and 484). Now part of the community, he must purify himself, just as they do. Previously, he did not fully belong to the world of the living. He was from the "water," was not yet "solid." He was a "thing," an "incomplete" being.

The vital fluids of the parents are like the elixir that gives the child the vigor lacking for him to take his place in society. But the anointing of the string is not fundamentally different from the purification of mourning. The sexual secretions are not a defilement in one case, and medicine in the other, but in both cases are simultaneously defilement and medicine. In effect, as soon as mourning is expelled, the spouses are purified by making the principle of defilement leave each of their bodies, without entering the body of the other spouse. But at the same time, they wet their navels with it, in order to take advantage of its energy. Again, it is with their vital fluids that they make an *aqueous* being *solid*, but by their not completing the sex act, they purify themselves. Junod emphasizes that the two rites must be explained in opposite ways, since the spouses are pure in one case, and impure in the other. But on the contrary, everything shows that they are no less contaminated by birth than by death. For it is only after the incomplete sex act that they wet their son's G-string with their "defilements" (besides, the word is very clear). Afterwards, they can have sexual intercourse again, since previously it had been strictly forbidden.

The order of things, in fact, forbids bringing a child into this semi-existence, while another is still dwelling in that kind of limbo which precedes life proper and which lasts from the moment of conception until the child is received into the circle of "big people," the truly living. Also the parents who conceived a child during this marginal period, in terms of a very meaningful expression, have "fled from the law." The child himself would never "enter the law." No matter how old he becomes, he is destined to be buried with foetuses and monsters, in the humid soil of the rejected. In fact, counting the time for gestation, it would be born before the weaning of the

older child, which takes place one year after the anointing of
the G-string. This definitely ends, because of the rite practiced
at the end of every serious illness, the time of weakness and
impurity that early childhood constitutes. A total purification
rids the youngster of every toxic miasma. His body is massaged
with various ingredients. He is rubbed with some bran, His
mother makes a small ball of the accumulated mixture containing all the poisons eliminated. She carries it into the forest and places it at the entrance to a large anthill, in such a
way that the ants must necessarily take it inside with them.
Then she returns without looking back. A single look would
be enough to return the malady to her children. It would re-
capture something of the defilement so carefully gathered together and banished. The ants now are responsible for leading
it back outside the world of health into the remote darkness
and the depths of the earth.

Moreover, the child is out of danger. Having left the
perilous margin, he no longer has to fear that his mother will
become pregnant again. If she had become pregnant before
he was weaned, before her milk had completely dried up, not
only would the second child have "barred the way," "blocked
the road," and would have outstripped him. Weakness and
paralysis would have been his lot.

The idea is obvious. As long as a physiological bond remains between mother and child (for example, the milk that
she feeds him), no one can interfere with their relationship
without running contrary to the normal development of life.
Everything that hurts the mother affects the child while their
absolute and vital independence is not assured by nature or
sanctioned by ritual. That is why a new pregnancy of the
mother prevents the growth of the child who has not yet won
full autonomy. Indeed, it *bars his way* by disturbing the kind
of closed economy that he and his mother form. There is no
room for two. The intruder *outstrips* him. He has arrived
while the place was still occupied. He has not waited the
interval required for the proper sequence of phenomena. A
creator of disorder, he is accursed, his life is a scandal and
transgression, and he has definitely harmed his brother.

Thus, everything happens as if there existed an *order of the universe* in which each thing must arrive in *its* place and time. It is extremely important that this order be respected. It is the very principle back of the conservation of the universe. Every violent phenomenon is an attack upon it. It is mainly the passages between this world and the other that risk upsetting an equilibrium, provoking the disorderly eruption of noxious powers, and dangerously mixing what must remain separate. That is why childbirth and death throes excite so much terror and make so many precautions necessary. They bring trouble. In particular, the defilement of death would then contaminate all if it were not destroyed by fire, removed by the flow of running water, or led back into the depths of the ground. The homes to which it came must be purified and sterilized by means of delicate and complicated operations, then everything is again calm and well-ordered.

The sex act liberates dreaded powers that encourage both good and bad influences, without distinction. It is heat and fire, that one must be able to temper with prudence in order to profit from it, without its being allowed to engulf and devour him.

Such is the sacred. It emanates from the dark world of sex and death, but it is the principle essential to life and the source of all efficacy. It is a force quick to discharge and difficult to isolate, always formidable, and simultaneously dangerous and indispensable. Ritual serves to capture, domesticate, and engage it in beneficial ways, and if need be, to neutralize its excessive acidity. At this stage religion is only the regulation of this omnipotent and invisible electric current that commands man's respect and, at the same time, invites him to possess it.

Appendix II—PLAY AND THE SACRED

OF ALL THE WORKS IN THE PHILOSOPHY OF HISTORY THAT
have appeared in this generation, one of the most mentally
stimulating is indisputably *Homo Ludens* by J. Huizinga.[36]
A keen and powerful intelligence, served by rare gifts of expression and exposition, compiles and interprets the services
rendered to culture by one of man's basic instincts, the one
that seems the most inappropriate to establish anything dur-
able or precious—that of play. In reading this book, one suddenly sees law, science, poetry, wisdom, war, philosophy, and
the arts enriched, occasionally originating, and always profit-
ing from the spirit of play. In fact, play stimulates or exercises,
as the case may be, the various faculties or desires that result
in producing civilization.

Huizinga's point of departure is the following definition,
the culmination of a masterly analysis:

> Summing up the formal characteristics of play, we might
> call it a free activity standing quite consciously outside "ordi-
> nary" life as being "not serious" but at the same time intensely
> and utterly absorbing the player. It is an activity connected
> with no material interest, and no profit can be gained by it.
> It proceeds within its own proper boundaries of time and
> space according to fixed rules and in an orderly manner. It
> promotes the formation of social groupings that tend to sur-
> round themselves with secrecy and to stress their difference
> from the common world by disguise or other means.[37]

The author completely avoids various biopsychological
explanations of play, such as discharge of excess energy, tend-

ency toward imitation, necessity for distraction, discipline for acquiring self-control, desire to enter into competition with others to prove one's superiority, innocuous sublimation of instincts forbidden direct satisfaction by society, etc. Huizinga rightly estimates that all these diverse conceptions are partial explanations, that no one of them accounts for the phenomenon in its entirety, and finally, that when, on occasion, one or another seems justified, they are mutually exclusive. In addition, he reproaches them more specifically. He makes the accusation that they equally presume a utilitarian goal for play activity. They attribute a biological or psychological function to play. In a word, they imply that play would be engaged in because it is advantageous for man. The theorist who wrote *Homo Ludens* sees in it, on the contrary, something purely superfluous. He deems its primary activity, a fundamental category that must be accepted as such, that can only be defined by its opposite (serious, ordinary, daily life), and consequently more susceptible to explaining than being explained.

In fact, proceeding from this immediate datum, Huizinga, in the course of his book, devotes himself to showing how

> The arena, the card-table, the magic circle, the temple, the stage, the screen, the tennis court, the court of justice, etc. are all in form and function play-grounds, i.e., forbidden spots, isolated, hedged round, hallowed, within which special rules obtain. All are temporary worlds within the ordinary world, dedicated to the performance of an act apart.[38]

These analyses are exceptionally vigorous and original. They almost always imply cohesion. One would have wished all the more to see the diverse mental attitudes underlying the different kinds of games better identified, such as skill, force, combination, chance, etc. One would have liked separate descriptions of each component of the gambling spirit, such as waiting for the die to be cast, the desire to prove one's superiority, the taste for competition or risk, the role of free improvization, the way in which it is related to respect for rules, etc. One point remains moot, however, is play truly one? Can a single term cover many activities that have only the name in common? Huizinga thinks so, and manifestly accords great importance to the philological proof for the basic identity of all play activity. However it is doubtful that this is sufficient proof.

In addition, the author is disturbed because the different kinds of play are not designated by the same word in all languages. However, the contrary would be surprising. It is evident that the Olympic Stadium and the gaming table imply for their devotees attitudes in which one can doubtless succeed in discovering common elements, but these do not have much bearing on the essential point. The athlete who merely takes chance into account, and the gambler who abandons himself to it, indubitably attest to states of mind as unrelated as possible. Here, it would seem, is the defect in this admirable work. It studies the external structures better than the intimate attitudes that give each activity its most precise meaning. And, the forms and rules of play are the object of more attentive examination than the needs satisfied by the game itself.

Such is truly the origin of the most daring thesis of the work, which is, in my sense, at the same time the most precarious—the identification of play and the sacred.

It is a delicate question, certainly more complex than it first seems, when an immediate impulse misguidedly inclines one to reject so paradoxical a connection for the sole reason that it runs counter to common sense. Certainly, believer and player, religion and play, temple and chessboard, seem to have nothing in common. There seems to be no doubt of this. But the author has scarcely shown how easily play can be joined to the serious. Examples are abundant and persuasive, to list a few, the child, the sportsman, and the actor. Let us omit the child since it is clear that for him play is the most serious thing in the world, although he can perfectly distinguish the imaginative role that he plays, when he calls a chair a horse, or a row of buttons an army ready for combat. Adults can do this as well when the stage or track is involved. Each sees that he expends energy within a determinate space and time, following more or less arbitrary conventions. Moreover, the serious is not absent from it. On the contrary, it is indispensible to it. Actors and spectators are excited to emulate each other.

So it is with religion, concludes Huizinga. The sanctuary, the church, and the liturgy fulfil an analogous function. An enclosed space is delimited, separated from the world and from life. In this enclosure, for a given time, regulated and symbolic movements are executed, which represent or reincarnate mysterious realities in the course of the ceremonies, in which, just as in play, the opposing qualities of exuberance and regimentation, of ecstasy and prudence, and of enthusiastic delirium and minute precision, are present at the same time. At last, one transcends ordinary existence.[39]

The author, following Jensen,[40] emphasizes above all, the state of mind of primitives at the time of their festivals, during which "ghosts" appear and wander about the assemblage. That is the climax of the religious fervor of these people. Moreover, the bystanders do not fear these "ghosts." Everyone, including the women, knows that they will be punished by death if they witness the preparations for the ceremony. Moreover, they know that it is their comrades, disguised and masked, who play this role. Again, at the time of the ordeals of initiation, it happens that the young warrior simulates a battle with a horrible monster, but it is obvious that he is confronting a crude effigy, painted, jointed, and moved by supernumeraries.

It is seen that play and the sacred are present, as if by connivance. Intense religious emotion is accompanied by a performance that is known to be artificial, by a spectacle that is knowingly played but that is in no way meant to be a deception or diversion.

This point has to be conceded, just as it is necessary to concede that the ritual order is a mere convention. In the profane world, it delimits a separate area ruled by a strict code and intended to obtain ideal results that have only the meaning or value that faith attributes to them. I can well imagine that if Huizinga, a medievalist, had been better informed in the findings of ethnography, he would have added many more arguments, à propos of strengthening his already solid case. Thus, many ordinary games have a sacred origin. Such are, for example, the game of string figures among the Eskimo, who establish the mystic pre-eminence of a seasonal principle by a natural element, marine or terrestial and linked with winter or summer. Examples are the stag beetles and greased poles which, in the Pacific, are related to myths of conquering the sky, and Maori ball games, akin to football, in which the ball represents the sun.

In this book, where I wished to illustrate the transiency of the sacred and the contagious mechanism of defilement, I found no better example than the quality of the one who is "it" in the children's game of tag.[41] It is also significant that this game and this very quality in Spanish are designated by precisely the same expression as that for defilement—*mancha.*

The mythology of the riddle would equally furnish appreciable support for Huizinga. He discusses it frequently, but as a battle of wits or a demonstration of ingenuity or knowledge, without being too concerned with its ritual function. The latter is, however, obvious in numerous cases. For challenges, tournaments, or riddle-contests, he found the best documentation in a monograph by Jan de Vries.[42] I have extracted only one episode from it the importance of which Dumézil, among others, has stressed.[43] In the Scandinavian sagas, in the reign of King Frey or Sigtrud (the texts are not in agreement), the execution of the aged is replaced by migrations of the young, similar to the Roman *ver sacrum.* It is decided upon after being challenged to perform difficult, impossible, or enigmatic tasks, from which a girl, counselled by the Goddess Frigga, emerges victorious. The tale is all the more remarkable in that it bears directly and clearly upon a reality of civilization.

The famous riddle that Samson proposes at a banquet should be recalled at this point. Finally, there seems to be no doubt that among primitives, as in more complex civilizations, riddles play a role in initiation rituals. The most famous of all, that solved by Oedipus which assured him the throne of Thebes, seems in any case to allude to a royal ordeal of initiation. A more important, and unexpected, instance could be that of the circus, of the antics of the clowns, and in particular the role of the *Auguste*,[44] whose activity consists of awry imitation and whose awkwardness or stupidity provokes burlesque catastrophes.

In myths, the intervention of a personage of the same type, such as the Trickster referred to by Anglo-Saxon scholars, is frequently observed. It is notably to his conduct, simultaneously ridiculous, inbecilic, and tragic in its consequences, that the origin of death is related when it is not attributed to the female. It can even be asked whether it may not be proper to interpret the presence of a joker in card games in the same way. The joker does not belong in the series, appearing in seemingly free and crazy combinations, mixing and completing them at the same time. Is this mere coincidence, or survival in hybrid form? It matters little for present purposes. The essential fact is that mythological material is rich and suggestive on this subject. What we have there, even more than for the *potlatch* from which it largely borrows, is a special opportunity for the author to show how an element in free play finds a place in the domain of the sacred. Besides, it is of interest that it is constantly found in legends which explain how man became mortal.

It is evident that I am the first to recognize the relationship that it is possible to establish between play and the sacred. Furthermore, I voluntarily carry grist to Huizinga's mill. But I part company with him on one decisive point. I do not believe that the various forms of play and of religion, because they are separated with equal care in daily life, occupy equivalent situations with respect to each other, nor that for this reason they are identical in content.

To be sure, that goes without saying, and I could be accused of breaking down doors that are already open. However, I believe that it is preferable to be precise. Debate is worthwhile, even if it is reduced to the interaction of tendencies. No one can deny that play is pure form, activity that is an end in itself, rules that are respected for their own sake. Huizinga himself stresses that its content is secondary.[45] This does not apply to the sacred, which, on the contrary, is pure content —an indivisible, equivocal, fugitive, and efficacious force.

Rites serve to capture, domesticate, and guide it, for better or worse. Compared to it, man's efforts remain precarious and uncertain, since by definition it is superhuman. He would be unable, in any case, to control it at his pleasure and confine its power to limits fixed in advance. Also, he must revive it, tremble in its presence, and supplicate it in humility. That is why the sacred has been defined as *tremendum* and *fascinans*. That is why prayer has been made the basic religious attitude, in contrast to the impious attitude of the magician who trys to constrain the forces that he employs.

Through the sacred, the source of omnipotence, the worshiper is fulfilled. Confronted by the sacred, he is defenseless and completely at its mercy. In play, the opposite is the case. All is human, invented by man the creator. For this reason, play rests, relaxes, distracts, and causes the dangers, cares, and travails of life to be forgotten. The sacred, on the contrary, is the domain of internal tension, from which it is precisely profane existence that relaxes, rests, and distracts. The situation is reversed.

In play, man is removed from reality. He seeks free activity, which does not involve him more than he has decided in advance. To begin with, he limits the consequences of his acts. He himself determines the stakes. He carefully demarcates the play area (arena, track, ring, stage, or chessboard) only in order to make it evident that it is a privileged space, ruled by special conventions in which acts have meaning only within that context. Outside this area, before and after play, one is no longer concerned with these arbitrary rules. The external, that is to say, life, is comparatively a kind of jungle in which a thousand perils await one. In my sense, the joy, abandon, and ease observed in play activity are derived from security. One knows that here things have only the importance that one has assigned to them. One can only be compromised by whatever one has consented to, and moreover, withdrawal is possible as soon as desired. How different is life! There, withdrawal in order to get out of a scrape, is rarely permitted. Difficulties, storms, unexpected and unwanted reverses must be confronted. At any given moment, one may become in-

volved more deeply than anticipated. And disloyalty is everywhere. It seems silly to respect rules and conventions, since it
no longer is a question of a game but of the struggle for existence.

In ordinary life, everyone is responsible for his acts. Mis-
takes, errors, and negligence are sometimes paid for dearly.
Therefore, one must always be careful of what one says or
does, for catastrophe may result. One knows that he who sows
the wind, reaps the tempest. Finally, mischance, accidents, in-
justices, and all too many undeserved misfortunes that can
attack the innocent, must also be reckoned with.

Play is not only the area of "limited and provisional per-
fection." It constitutes a kind of haven in which one is master
of destiny. There, the player himself chooses his risks, which,
since they are determined in advance, cannot exceed what he
has exactly agreed to put into play. These conditions are valid
chiefly in games of chance. To be sure, the player can surrender himself to destiny, but he himself decides to what degree.
Also, he is freer and more independent in play than in life, and
in one sense he is less vulnerable to bad luck. If he stakes all
his means at once, no one has forced him to, and if he loses,
he has nothing to blame but his own passion.

What is a good player? Someone who takes into account
that he has no right to complain of bad luck nor to grieve
about a misfortune, the possibility of which he has deliberately
accepted if not courted. In a word, a good player is one who
possesses sufficient equanimity not to confuse the domains of
play and life. He is one who shows, even when he loses, that
for him, play remains play, that is to say, a pastime to which
he does not accord importance unworthy of someone well-
loved, and he regards it as indecent to be crushed by its risks.

Thus, one is led to define play as a free activity in which
man finds himself immune to any apprehension regarding
his acts. He defines its impact. He establishes its conditions
and conclusion. From this derives his ease, calm, and good
humor, which are not merely natural but even obligatory. It
is a point of honor with him not to show that he takes the
game too seriously, even in the event of ruin or defeat.

Is it necessary to recall that the sacred involves entirely opposite laws? Its domain is no less scrupulously separated from profane life, but that is in order to protect the latter from its terrible onslaughts, not because the shock of the real would instantly destroy it as if it were a fragile convention. Without doubt, the control of the sacred power is not capricious. To tame such dreadful forces, meticulous precautions are necessary. Only a masterly technique will succeed. Proven formulae, charms, and passwords authorized and taught by God himself are needed. They are performed and pronounced in imitation of Him, and owe their efficaciousness to Him. In effect, one has recourse to the sacred in order to influence real life, to assure victory, prosperity, and all the desirable results of divine favor. The power of the sacred transcends ordinary life. In leaving the temple, or after making a sacrifice, man is restored to liberty, and to a more clement atmosphere in which acts, accomplished without fear or trembling, lead less infallibly to inexpiable results.

In sum, one feels as relaxed in passing from sacred activity to profane life, as when passing from profane preoccupation and vicissitudes to the climate of play.[46] In both cases, one's behavior earns a new degree of liberty. It is a fact that the ideas of the free and the profane are expressed by the same word in many languages. In this sense, play, free activity par excellance, is the pure profane, has no content, does not connote on other levels any result that was not permissible to avoid. In relation to life, it is only pleasure and diversion. It is life, on the contrary, that is vanity and diversion, in contrast to the sacred. Therefore, a *sacred-profane-play* hierarchy needs to be established in order to balance Huizinga's analysis. The sacred and play resemble each other to the degree that they are both opposed to the practical life, but they occupy symmetrical situations with regard to it. Play must dread it. It breaks or dissipates play at the first collision. Conversely, one believes that it depends upon the sovereign power of the sacred.

The author so broadens the definition of play that finally every regulated, conventional, or gratuitous form is included. His formula even absorbs the military arts, prosody, and legal procedure. It is not surprising that he then finds in the sacred manifestations of the same instinct that he so brilliantly related in various ways to the development of culture. I have already indicated that this approach is a fertile one, which can yield even more astonishing discoveries. It is no less true that even if the forms are comparable, the contents vary in each instance. The military arts do not explain war, neither does prosody explain poetry, nor does law explain the requirements of justice.[47] The same is true for the sacred. I know that it is separated from the routine world, that all acts performed there are regulated and symbolic, that the priest dons ceremonial vestments and plays a role, and finally I know that the entire liturgy is something of a game. However, if one considers not merely its forms, but the intimate attitudes of the officiant and of the faithful, I also see that sacrifice and communion are involved, that one is then fully in the sacred, and as far removed from play as is conceivable.

I would like to add a final word. *Homo Ludens* ends with a bitter chapter on the decadence of the play-element in modern times. Perhaps this is only an optical illusion of a *laudator temporis acti*. One has to be skeptical, but it is impossible to mistake the alarming regression of the sacred and of festivals in modern society. It is a world that is not sacred, without festivals, without play, therefore, without fixed moorings, without devotional principles, without creative license, a world in which immediate interest, cynicism, and the negation of every norm not only exist, but are elevated into absolutes in place of the rules that underlie all play, all noble activity, and honorable competition. One should not be surprised to meet there few things that do not lead to war.

Because of the wishes of those who attack every code as merely a convention or restraint, it is no longer a question of war as a tournament but war as violence, no longer a matter of ordeals in which the strong measure their valor and skill but of implacable hostilities in which the most numerous and the best armed crush and massacre the weak. Even in war and the very heart of combat, there is culture, so that the loss or rejection of the play-element does not at all lead to pure and simple barbarism. There is no civilization without play and rules of fair play, without conventions consciously established and freely respected. There is no culture in which knowing how to win or lose loyally, without reservations, with self-control in victory, and without rancor in defeat, is not desired. One wants to be *en beau joueur*. Finally, there is no morality, no mutual confidence, no respect for others—conditions for any thriving enterprise—and their underlying sacred commandments, which no one risks discussing, and for the safe-guarding of which each thinks that it is worth the sacrifice of his own life and, if need be, the risk of the very survival of the community of which he is a part.

It should not be forgotten that worse than the cheat is the one who disdains or refuses to play, ridiculing the rules or exposing their vanity. Huizinga tells of the Shah of Persia who, invited to England to attend the Derby, asked to be excused by saying that he already knew that one horse runs faster than another. It is the same for the sacred. Nothing is more destructive of culture than these "wet blankets," who are skeptics and doubters. They like to smile at everything, naively believing that they thus affirm their superiority. Through vanity, they only cause injury to a precious treasure that was accumulated, at the cost of infinite pains. At least they might be iconoclastic and sacrilegious in the idea of establishing in their turn the rules of a new game that is more pleasant or more serious.

Appendix III—WAR AND THE SACRED

THE FESTIVAL, PAROXYSM OF PRIMITIVE SOCIETY

By CONTEMPLATING THE PLACE HELD BY MYTHS IN SOCIEties in which they completely dominate men's imagination and determining through rites the acts essential to their survival, one is persuaded that some reality must immutably assure their functioning in societies where myths are not so regarded. They are not easy to conceal, for they must involve important deeds and sufficient faith to make them seem necessary or natural in a way that would not conflict in the least with denouncing as mythical those powerful beliefs, and convince the adherents of a religion, whose creed demands the most serious conformity, that they are absurd superstitions. That is to say, myth will be found even where it is at first regarded as repugnant, as soon as one seeks it in its proper milieu.

Accompanying myths is the festival, a periodic effervescence that stirs primitive societies from top to bottom. It is a phenomenon of such duration, violence, and magnitude, that it can only be broadly compared to days of pleasure with no thought for the morrow in complex civilizations. One thinks erroneously of vacations, but these are soon revealed, not as the equivalent, but rather as the contrary of ancient merrymaking. In fact, they do not produce meaningful interruptions or transformations in collective life. They do not connote the period of massed assembling of the populace, but rather of their dispersion far from urban centers, of their finding diversion in peripheral solitude and wide open spaces, toward regions of least tension. Vacations do not represent a crisis, climax, or moment of major precipitation and participation, but a time of slackening and relaxation. They demarcate a dead time in the rhythm of general activity. Finally, they restore the individual to himself, rid him of his cares and his work, exempt him from his official duties, rest and isolate him. The festival, by contrast, uproots him from his privacy and his personal or familial world in order to throw him into the whirlpool in which a frenzied multitude noisily affirms its oneness and indivisibility by expending all its wealth and power at one stroke. From any point of view, vacations, an empty and absent interlude, appear to be the opposite of this furious exuberance in which a society is reinvigorated.

It is necessary to seek and find the replica of such a paroxysm, a reality of different mass and tension, than can truly serve as the climax of existence for modern society, to elevate and bring it to a kind of glowing transformation.

It is, therefore, appropriate to recall the characteristics of the primitive festival. It is a time of excess. Reserves accumulated over the course of several years are squandered. The holiest laws are violated, those that seem at the very basis of social life. Yesterday's crime is now prescribed, and in place of customary rules, new taboos and disciplines are established, the purpose of which is not to avoid or soothe intense emotions, but rather to excite and bring them to climax. Movement increases, and the participants become intoxicated. Civil or administrative authorities see their powers temporarily diminish or disappear. This is not so much to the advantage of the regular sacerdotal caste as to the gain of secret confraternities or representatives of the other world, masked actors personifying the Gods or the dead. This fervor is also the time for sacrifices, even the time for the sacred, a time outside of time that recreates, purifies, and rejuvenates society. Next take place ceremonies that fertilize the soil and promote the adolescent generation to the grade of men and warriors. All excesses are permitted, for society expects to be regenerated as a result of excesses, waste, orgies, and violence. It hopes for new vigor to come out of explosion and exhaustion. One can scarcely find in complex and machine civilizations a single equivalent of this crisis that cuts brutally into the monotonous heart of daily life, that is so extremely in contrast to it. However, taking into account the nature and development of modern society, only one phenomenon manifests comparable importance, intensity, and explosiveness, of the same order of grandeur—*war*.

WAR, PAROXYSM OF MODERN SOCIETY

Any other phenomenon seems indeed to be ridiculously out of proportion before the immense mobilization of energy represented by the festival, wherever it exists in full force. It is necessary to go on, therefore, despite the implausibility and scandalousness of such a correlation, and agree to examine it a little closer. Without doubt, war is horror and catastrophe, the inundation of death, and the festival is consecrated to outbursts of joy and super-abundance of life. But there is no pretense here of comparing their meaning or content, but rather their absolute grandeur, their function in collective life, the image they imprint on the individual's mind—in a word, the place they hold rather than the manner in which they occupy it. If war corresponds to the festival, it will be all the more instructive, when it appears to be its opposite, and the investigation of their differences will serve to specify and supplement the conclusions inspired by their confirmed similarities.

War and The Festival

War well represents a paroxysm in the life of modern society. It constitutes a total phenomenon that exalts and transforms modern society in its entirety, cutting with terrible contrast into the calm routine of peacetime. It is a phase of extreme tension in collective life, a great mobilization of masses and effort. Each individual is torn from his profession, his home, his habits, and lastly, his leisure. War brutally destroys the circle of liberty that everyone preserves for his own pleasure and respects in his neighbor. It interrupts the happiness and quarrels of lovers, the intrigue of the ambitious, and the work quietly pursued by the artist, scholar or inventor. It impartially ruins anxiety and placidity, and nothing exists that may not be taken away by war, whether creation, pleasure, or even anguish. No one can remain apart from it and busy himself with another task, for there is no one whom war cannot employ in some fashion. It needs all energies.

Therefore, following the kind of partioning in which each arranges his life as he wishes, without participating much in civic affairs, there comes a time in which society unites all its members in a collective movement, which suddenly places them side by side, assembles, arranges, aligns, and welds them together, body and soul. The hour has come at which society brusquely ceases being tolerant and indulgent and is anxious to have people, whose prosperity she protects, forget this. Society now takes possession of property, and demands the time, labor, and even the blood of its citizens. Their uniforms are a visible sign that they have abandoned everything that distinguished peacetime in order to serve the community not as they would wish, but in terms of whatever their uniforms command them to do, and at the posts designated.

The similarity of war and the festival is absolute, therefore, in these respects. Both inaugurate a period of vigorous socialization and share instruments, resources, and powers in common. They interrupt the time during which individuals separately occupy themselves in very many different domains. In their turn, they depend upon one another and mutually overlap rather than occupy a definite place in a strict system. In modern society, for this reason, war represents a unique moment of concentration and intense absorption in the group of everything that ordinarily tends to maintain a certain area of independence in this regard. That is why in preference to vacations and holidays, it calls for comparison with the ancient season of collective effervescence.

A TIME OF EXCESS, VIOLENCE, AND OUTRAGE

The festival is in the same relationship to the time of labor, as war is to peace. They are both phases of movement and excess, as against the phases of stability and moderation. *Quieta non movere,* the maxim of regulated existence, is also that of peaceful diplomacy. Their common quality compels them to make allowance always for a possible conflagration. Conversely, surprise, violence, brusqueness, and skill in concentrating or putting in motion the greatest possible forces at one point are simple strategies that are as valid for the festival as for war. Each has its own discipline, but both seem nevertheless like monstrous and shapeless explosions against the monotonous routine of ordinary life.

In addition, ordinary life is composed only of detailed approximations. Its equilibrium and tranquility are the result of a host of minute, anarchic errors that do not entail consequences that are too alarming, and whose effects reciprocally cancel each other. The only hindrance lies in how it is commonly conceived, for despite the rigors of military arts and ceremonial, war and the festival remain images of disorder and confusion.

In primitive groups, the highest law upon which the social order is founded is the rule of exogamy; in modern society, it is respect for another's life. If one takes life in ordinary times, he is exposed to the severest sanctions and the most indignant reproof. But when the hour for combat or the dance arrives, new norms emerge. Acts hitherto prohibited and deemed abominable now carry glory and prestige, provided that they are performed within the limits of a kind of etiquette accompanied by ritual practices designed to sanctify or disguise them, although they may be performed in an undisciplined unleashing of raging instincts. It is not only the killing of the enemy that is honored in war, but the entirety of acts and attitudes that blames morality itself upon civilian life, acts and attitudes forbidden to the child by its parents and to the adult by public opinion and laws. Tricks and lies are appreciated. Even robbery is permissible. When necessities have to be procured or even a simple supplement to a pittance, one is not too particular about the means used, and, moreover, ingenuity is more highly esteemed than scruples. As for the kill-

ing itself, one knows that one is forced to do it, that it is a re-
payment, and is required.

JOY OF DESTRUCTION

Finally, from everywhere the long-inhibited joy of destruction springs forth, the pleasure of leaving an object
shapeless and unrecognizable, the voluptuousness known by
the doctor in exciting himself over a little thing until he has
converted it into nameless debris, in a word, all liberating violence of which man is deprived since he no longer has toys
that he can break as soon as they no longer please. He goes to
break the dishes that have just been bought. This is paltry
satisfaction, as against the intoxication of killing. Pleasure
seems greatest for man when he vanquishes his fellow man.
If he abandons himself to it, it sometimes leaves him panting
and faint. He admits and boasts of it.[48]

A furor seizes the warrior in which he believes himself
possessed by a primary instinct buried deep in his heart by a
lying civilization. "When in an orgy of fury, the true man
compensates for his continence! Instincts too long repressed
by society and its laws once again become basic—holy object
and highest reason."[49]

Like incest in the festival, killing in war is an act of religious impact. It is related to human sacrifice, it is said, and
has no immediate utility. That is exactly how the popular
mind distinguishes it from criminal killing. The same law
that requires the soldier to sacrifice his life orders him to im-
molate his enemy. The rules of warfare vainly try to make a
noble game out of it, a kind of duel in which violence is
limited by loyalty and courtesy. But the essential part is to
kill. The requirement is always to annihilate properly the
enemy, like game on a hunt; to destroy him, if possible, when
he is discovered asleep and unarmed. The good general is
not the one who risks his men gratuitously. Some thinkers
have estimated that modern war, in which the civilian is not
spared and in which great agglomerations furnish wide tar-
gets, easy to attack with certain damage, for the most mur-

derous enemy onslaughts, best conforms to the ideal essence
of war. The true warrior expects to see suppressed the chivalric code, that in other times made battles seem like grand
tournaments. He is not at all displeased that in this festival
the role of liturgy diminishes and that of license and orgies
increases.

SACRILEGE AND WASTE

Most awesome fears concern death. It is an object of the
greatest respect. The presence of a corpse entails silence and
removing one's hat. War—which makes for extreme familiarity with the remains of the slain that one has not even had
the opportunity to bury—on the contrary, develops a friendly
casualness in this regard.[50] One jokes and speaks to them, and
pats them with the hand in passing. The impertinence succeeds in constraining death. The miserable remains are
kicked aside and scoffed at by word and deed, so as not to become afraid of them or to avoid becoming obsessed by them.
A laugh is a shield against chill. Man is newly freed from the
taboos imposed upon him by custom and education. There
is an end to bowing before the dead and honoring them, while
concealing their horrible reality to the eye as well as to the
mind. It exists unadorned, with nothing glossing it over or protecting it. It is the hour in which one can pillage and soil this
greatly revered object, the mortal remains of man. Who would
deprive himself of such a revenge and profanation? In the end,
everything deemed sacred is reclaimed by death. At the same
time that it causes trembling, it wants to be defiled and spat at.

The festival is the occasion for immense waste. Reserves
accumulated for months, and sometimes for years, are squandered. War does not correspond in the least to prodigality.
There are no longer mountains of food or lakes of drink, for
war is concerned with an entirely different kind of consumption. Thousands of tons of projectiles are used each day. Ar-
senals are emptied as rapidly as granaries. Just as all disposable
foods are amassed for the festival, so loans, levies, and requisi-

tions drain the varied riches of a country and throw them into the abyss of war, which absorbs them without ever being amassed. Here the food consumed in one day by the multitude would be sufficient for a whole season's festival, for even the figures make one dizzy. The cost of several hour's hostilities represents such a considerable sum that one could believe it possible to put an end to the misery of the whole world with it. In both cases, non-productive, brutal, and almost insane exhaustion of resources is observed—resources that have been gathered by dint of privation and labor in order that in the end avarice is suddenly succeeded by prodigality.

War thus reflects a cluster of entirely external characteristics, which suggests that it be regarded as the modern and somber counterpart of the festival. One ought not be surprised that, as soon as it became a political institution, it was accompanied by an ideology that tended to exalt it, like the state, as a kind of cosmic and fertile principle. The contents of war and the festival are opposed in vain, since the analogies of form and mass are such that the imagination is vague about identifying their nature.

The Mystique of War

WAR, THE MILESTONE OF TIME

Festivals open the doors to the world of the Gods, and man is transformed into a God and attains superhuman existence. They border on the dream-time, and serve to demarcate the time for work. The calendar, between festivals, counts only empty and anonymous days, which only exist as related to their more expressive days. Even today, when festivals have lost almost all reality, one still says, it is after Easter, or it was before Christmas. War also seems like a milestone in the passage of time. It cuts across the life of nations. Each time it inaugurates a new era. An age ends when war begins. And when it ends, a new age begins that differs in very obvious respects from the first. Life is no longer lived the same way. After the war, the nation recovers from the ordeal, or from preparing for it. All is relaxation or tension. Also the prewar periods are carefully distinguished from the postwar periods. Primitive peoples, among whom war is chronic and small-scale, live the same way, observers report, but in relation to the festival, that is, in the recollection of the past festival or in anticipation of the next festival. For the rest, one passes from one to the other attitude by imperceptible steps. The transition from postwar to prewar is no less gradual. The change is effected psychologically, politically, and economically at the same time. Peacetime is neutral. It lends itself to contrary orientations and constitutes a kind of stop-gap between two crises. From this at first arises the prestige of war, which little by little balances, then removes the terrors that it provokes.

It can be considered as an absurd and criminal catastrophe. Man's honor appears to deny it. The first goal of his efforts is to avoid it. But soon he comes to regard war as inevitable. It grows to the stature of destiny. It takes on the dignity of a frightful natural scourge, spreading ruin and devastation, and while intelligence still condemns it, the heart respects it like every power that man places or recognizes as beyond his control. This reverence is only a beginning. Inevitably, the mortal who will be its victim comes to regard war as necessary. He sees it as chastisement by God, if he is a theologian, and he approves of Joseph de Maistre. He discovers in it the law of nature or the moving force of history, if he is a philosopher, and so he follows Hegel. It no longer comes into the world accidentally, but as the very norm of the universe. It becomes the essential mechanism of the cosmos, and as such gains a decidedly religious value. Its benefits are extolled. It is no longer barbarism, but the source and most beautiful flower of civilization. Everything is created by war, and peace causes everything to perish through engulfment and erosion. Wars are necessary to regenerate societies and save them from death, to preserve them from the effects of irretrievable time. The quality of the fountain of youth is lent to these blood baths.

WAR, A REGENERATIVE POWER

One recognizes the powers commonly attributed to festivals. Through them too, the periodic rejuvenation of society was sought. One intended to cull, in celebrating them, a new era of vigor and health. Even by its vocabulary, the mythology of war permits a correlation with the festival. War is made into a Goddess of tragic fertility. It is compared to a gigantic childbirth. And just as the mother risks her life in giving birth to a child, peoples must pay a bloody tribute in order to establish or perpetuate their existence. "War is the most elemental form of love for life."[51] It reinterprets the law of the birth of nations and corresponds to the visceral movements of nature, necessarily horrible, that are prominent in physical births. Neither will nor intelligence has any control over war, just as if they tried to govern the work of the intestines. Moreover, these devastating convulsions reveal to man the value and power of the more subterranean energies. They uproot him from the ignoble stagnation of peace in which he vegetates, attached to a degrading tranquility, and desiring to attain the basest ideal —security in property. War shatters a paralyzed and moribund order and forces man to construct a new future over great and frightful ruins.[52]

From then on, how can one see in war the last recourse of despair, the ultimate argument of kings, the severe and dreadful necessity to which he must indeed resign himself, when all other means have failed? It is more than a frightful remedy in which nations are sometimes constrained to seek safety. It constitutes their reason for being. It even serves to define them. The nation is all men who wage war side by side. And in its turn, war defines the supreme expression of the desire for national existence. It constitutes the highest moral commandment for peoples. War must not serve as a foundation for peace, but peace must serve as preparation for war since peace is only a simple and transitory armistice between two conflicts.[53] All valuable effort is oriented toward war and finds its conservation in it. All else is contemptible that has no utility for war. "All human and social destiny is justified, only if it prepares for war."[54]

WAR, A SACRAMENT

This state of mind is authentically religious. War, no less than the festival, seems like the time of the sacred, the period of the divine epiphany. It introduces man to an intoxicating world in which the presence of death makes him shiver and confers a superior value upon his various actions. He believes that he will acquire a psychic vigor—just as through the descent to the inferno in ancient initiations—out of proportion to mundane experiences. He feels invincible and as if marked by the sign that protected Cain after the murder of Abel. "We have plunged into the heart of life in order to re-emerge completely transformed."[55] It seems that war makes the combatants drink long draughts until the very dregs of a fatal philter that it alone dispenses, transforming their conception of existence. "Today we can affirm that we have conquered, we soldiers of the front, the basis of life and discovered the very essence of our being."[56]

War, a new divinity, then wipes out sins and bestows grace. Sovereign virtues are attributed to baptism by fire. It is imagined that the individual thus becomes the deserving hero of a tragic cult and the chosen one of a jealous God. Among those who together receive this consecration, or share the dangers of battle side by side, is born the fraternity of arms. Enduring ties unite these warriors henceforth. They are given a feeling of superiority and complicity at the same time toward those who have remained out of danger and who have not even played an active role in combat. It is not sufficient to have been exposed, it is necessary to have been attacked. The sacred is double. It implies that one dares not only to die but even to kill. A stretcher-bearer has no prestige. Combatants are not equal, for this status comprises various degrees. Different weapons from air power to commissariat, front line zones of operation to rear echelons, distinctions obtained, wounds, mutilations—anything may constitute hierarchical initiations and furnish a pretext for associations dedicated to glorifying them. They are something like the men's societies that, among primitives, one enters after painful ordeals and whose members enjoy special privileges throughout the community.

TOTAL WAR

The modern world, by its very nature, uneasily tolerates these professionals in violence. It eliminates the species, although it re-emerges as soon as circumstances are favorable. But even if the new structure of society and the mechanized or scientific form of combat substitutes countless and anonymous combatants for the traditional hero, the old attitude has not been modified. The necessity for discipline and the means to apply it rigorously doubtless limit the fantastic excesses of the past, but war ceaselessly gains in magnitude what it loses in instinctive release. Thus, it acquires another characteristic of the festival—its total nature. Combat begins to involve masses, and conquest is sought at least cost. Also it strikes at the weak. Tactics shun the armed encounter between equals. It is far removed from the duel and is akin to assassination and the hunt. One attempts to surprise an adversary inferior in number and weapons, in order to be sure of crushing him, while remaining invisible and immune, if possible. More and more, war is waged at night and by means of the reciprocal massacre of unarmed populations whose work provides supplies for the combatants.

There is no longer a well-defined battlefield, which used to constitute a reserved area, comparable to the lists, the arena, and the playing field. This enclosure, dedicated to violence, at least left all around it a world ruled by more clement laws. War, from now on, extends to the entire national territory. It also goes on indefinitely. Hostilities no longer commence after a solemn declaration fixing the moment at which firing begins. Attack is sudden, in order to take decisive advantage of a stunned adversary. Space or time consecrated to a gigantic duel are, therefore, no longer limited and separated from other time or space, so that it is no longer an ordeal set off at an agreed signal and in proper bounds.

Simultaneously, the progressive elimination of every chivalric or regulated element is observed. War becomes in some way purified and reduced to its perfect essence. It becomes stripped of every element foreign to its true being and is liberated from the hybrid marriage contracted with the spirit of play and competition. War, which is "pure crime and violation,"[57] had most paradoxically accepted loyalty, respect for the enemy, and had outlawed the use of certain weapons, ruses, and tactics, had established a complicated ceremonial and rigorous etiquette in which one applied himself to emulation in good manners as well as bravery and audacity.

RELATION BETWEEN THE PRESTIGE AND THE HORROR OF WAR

This sordid and massive war, greedy and needy, requires the hardest sacrifices of the individual without paying him anything in exchange. It consumes him without offering any compensation. It seems to be more and more reduced to a simple and implacable test of strength, to competitive emulation in lies and brutality. War is also the moment in which he becomes more and more exalted. It is regarded as a supreme benefit for mankind, and as the very principle of the universe. Never was its prestige so persuasive, never did it excite so much lyricism and religious enthusiasm. It attracts in proportion to the renunciations that it imposes and the abjection it assumes.

It should not be surprising that war is related to the passions. They seem more faithful to their nature, more grandiose and idyllic, when there is nothing that inhibits them. Again, when war loses all moderation, mobilizes the energies of a people, expends, without counting, the resources of a great nation, when it violates every rule and every law, when it has ceased even in part to resemble anything human—it is then that war appears to wear the most luminous halo. Crushing generations under gigantic ruins, burning with the somber brilliance of an immense conflagration, it well appears to be the dreadful paroxysm of collective life. Nothing can challenge the sinister glory of being the only event in modern society that uproots individuals from their particular caves in order to suddenly precipitate them into another world in which they no longer have a place and in which they find mourning, grief, and death.

The greater the contrast between the sweetness of peace

and the hideous violence of war, the greater the chance in war of seducing a band of fanatics and frightening enough others, so that, defenseless against it, they recognize in it some kind of fatal virtue that paralyzes them. That is why the quasi-mystical exaltation of war coincides with the moment in which its most striking horror is attained. One would first joke about it, deem it a pleasant occupation, or one would even curse the misery, suffering, and ruin that it entailed. But war will only make for giddiness on the day when, freed of every moral limitation, and no longer sparing anything or anyone, it will be manifested as a kind of cataclysm, inconceivable and unbearable, but of years' duration, extending to the very ends of the civilized world.

The magnitude of the event, its extension in time and space, its exceptional intensity, its brutal character, and its purely violent nature is finally clear after the rejection of lace uniforms and court ceremonials. That is what flatters their chilled hearts and persuades them that it opens the doors of an inferno for them that is truer and braver than a happy life without a sense of history. They distinguish from it the dreadful manifestation of the principle from which everything develops, and which reveals their true being. War is baptism and ordination, as much as it is apotheosis. On the rubbish of an illusory and corrupt world, weak, tarnished, and false at the same time, war proclaims and illustrates, with the apparatus and fracas of its nature's great rages, death's sacred triumph that so often in the past obsessed men's imaginations.

WAR, DESTINY OF NATIONS

It is understood that war is no less exciting. It plays the role of the ancient merrymaking quite well. It reminds the individual that he is not master of his destiny and that the higher powers on which he depends suddenly uproot him from his tranquility, and crush him at will. War truly seems to be the goal for which nations have been feverishly preparing. At the same time, it orients their efforts and their destiny. It seems to them the supreme ordeal that qualifies or disqualifies them for a new era. For war demands everything—wealth, resources, and lives—which it unrestrainedly squanders.

War offers satisfaction to the instincts that are opposed to civilization and that, under its patronage, take a glorious revenge, total annihilation and destruction. Dedicated to wastefulness and capable of engulfing whatever has form and identity, war results in a dual and sumptuous release for life that is tired of petty prohibitions and prudent refinements. A monstrous societal brew and climax of existence, a time of sacrifice but also of violation of every rule, a time of mortal peril but yet sanctifying, a time of abnegation and also of license—war has every right to take the place of the festival in the modern world and to excite the same fascination and fervor. It is inhuman, and it is sufficient to be deemed divine. Nothing is lacking. And one anticipates the most potent ecstasy, youth, and immortality from its sacred character.

EXCHANGE OF FUNCTIONS BETWEEN WAR AND THE FESTIVAL

In contrast to festivals, wars in primitive society, lack impressiveness and magnitude and cut a poor figure. They are merely brief interludes, expeditions for hunting, raiding, or vengeance. They constitute a permanent state that forms the fabric of basic existence. No doubt they are a dangerous occupation, but their continuity deprives them of any exceptional character. The festival interrupts hostilities. It temporarily reconciles the worst enemies, causing them to fraternize in the same effervescence. Even in antiquity, the Olympic Games suspended quarrels, and the entire Greek world communed in the temporary merrymaking protected by the Gods.

In modern society, the opposite occurs. War stops everything, and competitions, merrymaking, and international expositions are the first to be stricken. War closes the frontiers that are opened by festivals. One again perceives that war inherits all the powers of the festival but uses them for a contrary purpose. It separates instead of uniting. The festival is above all a uniting factor. Observers have recognized in the

festival a social bond par excellence, one that above all assures
the cohesion of the groups it assembles periodically. It unites
them in joy and delirium, without counting that the festival
is at the same time the occasion for dietary, economic, sexual,
and religious exchange, just as it is the occasion for rivalry in
prestige, symbols, heraldry, feats of strength and skill, reciprocal ritual gifts, dances, and talismans. It renews agreements and
rejuvenates unions.

In return, war provokes breach of contract and friendship.
It exasperates opposition. Not only is it an inexhaustible
source of death and devastation, while the festival manifests an
exuberance of life and fertile vigor, but the consequences of
war are no less fatal than the ravages that it causes while it is
rife. Its effects endure after its malevolent work is over. They
cause rancor and hate to fester and grow. Other misfortunes
result from it, and in the end there is a new war, which re-
sumes from where the preceding war left off. By contrast, at
the end of a festival, the date for the next one has already been
fixed in order to perpetuate and renew its benefits. The bad
seed of war is no less prompt to germinate. A worse fatality of
evils grows up to replace the cycle of fertile tumult.

WAR, THE RANSOM OF CIVILIZATION

What are the causes of such a reversal? How is it that great
social upheavals set generous forces into motion in one place,
and avaricious forces in another, on the one hand, reinforcing
communion, on the other hand, deepening division, at one
point an act of creative superabundance, at another point an
act of murderous fury? It is difficult to say. Doubtless, this contrast corresponds to the structural differences that exist between the organization of a primitive tribe and that of a modern nation.

Must it be the fault of industrial civilization and the
mechanization of collective life? Or is it the fault of the
gradual disappearance of the domain of the sacred, under the
pressure of profane mentality, harsh and greedy, necessarily
destined to pursue material profit by the simple means of vio-

lence and trickery? Or is it attributable to the formation of strongly centralized states at a time when the development of science and its applications makes it easy to govern vast multitudes that can suddenly be made to move with precision and efficiency previously inconceivable? We do not know. It is vain to choose an explanation. In any case, it is clear that the excessive swell of modern war and the mystique of which it is the object, are contemporary with these three orders of phenomena, successively bound to them, and besides furnishing abundant counterparts.

The problem of techniques, and consequently of means of control and coercion, the victory of the secular over the religious spirit, and in general the pre-eminence of mercenary over disinterested activity, the establishment of immense nations in which those in power always leave less liberty to the individual and are led to assign him a most strictly limited place in a most complex mechanism—such are indeed the fundamental transformations of societies, without which war could not be present in its actual character as absolute paroxysm of collective existence. There are those who would assure it the character of a black festival, apotheosis in reverse. Some regard it as fascinating for the religious part of the human mind. The mind trembles in horror and ecstasy to see in war the triumph of the powers of death and destruction in unexceptionable fashion.

This terrible ransom paid for the various advantages of civilization causes them to pale and proclaims their fragility. Before the convulsion that seizes them, as if they were without substance or depth, the results of an effort that is misguided, that scarcely seems to be compatible with nature, are apparent. There is no doubt that war rouses or flatters energies once ancient and basic, pure, if so desired, and true. But there are powers that man tries hard to conquer. The substitution of war for the festival perhaps is a measure of the road he has traveled from his original condition, and tears and blood perhaps are the price he must pay for conquests of all kinds, that he believes he is capable of undertaking.

Of late, man has learned, as the poet says, to draw "a terrible spark out of the fire-place of power." This furnishes arms
at a price to the two empires, each of which dominates a con-
tinent. Is the mastery of atomic energy, joined to the division
of the world between two giant states, sufficient to transform
radically the nature and conditions of war in such a way as to
render any comparison between war and the festival obsolete?
Nothing of the kind. One would only be able to escape the
prodigious increase in power that is man's lot, and balance it,
as previously, with a peril of equal magnitude. A peril that
appears to threaten the very existence of the species. Also, it
seems susceptible to even greater consecration. The prospect
of a kind of total festival, which threatens to drag nearly the
entire population of the globe into its whirlpool and to annihilate the majority of its participants, now proclaims the advent of a powerful catastrophe—frightening, paralyzing, and,
in addition, of greater prestige.

Reality is joined to fable. It attains cosmic dimensions,
and is revealed to be capable of executing the most important
decisions. Today, a myth of general annihilation like that of
the Twilight of the Gods no longer belongs solely to the domain of the imagination. The festival was the creation of the
imagination. It was facsimile, dance, and play. It pantomimed
the destruction of the universe, in order to assure its periodic
restoration. To consume everything, to leave each one panting
and as if dead, was a sign of vigor, a gauge of abundance and
longevity. It would no longer be the same. The day in which
energy was liberated in a sinister paroxysm, disproportionate
in grandeur and power to the relative fragility of life, would
definitely break the equilibrium in favor of destruction. This
excess of seriousness in the festival would make it fatal not
only for men, but perhaps also for itself. Moreover, it would
basically demarcate only the last step in the evolution that
transforms this explosion of life into war.

BIBLIOGRAPHY

N. B.—This bibliography is not meant to be complete or systematic. Only those works are cited which have been directly relevant to this book, or have influenced the author in his methodology, even though in certain cases their conclusions could not be reconciled with his own.*

E. Durkheim, *Elementary Forms of the Religious Life* (Glencoe, Illinois: Free Press, 1950)

P. D. Chantepie de la Saussaye, *Manuel d'histoire des religions* (Paris, 1904)

R. Otto, *Idea of the Sacred* (New York: Oxford University Press, 2nd Edition, 1950)

J. G. Frazer, *The Golden Bough* (London, 3rd Edition, 1925)

F. B. Jevons, *Introduction to the History of Religion* (London, 1896)

A. H. Krappe, *The Science of Folklore* (New York, 1930)

A. Vierkandt, "Das heilige in den primitiven Religionen," *Die Dioshuren*, 1922

A. Van Gennep, *Tabou et totémisme à Madagascar* (Paris, 1904)

M. Mauss, *Gift—Forms and Functions of Exchange in Archaic Societies* (Glencoe, Illinois: Free Press, 1954)

M. J. Lagrange, *Etudes sur les religions sémitiques* (Paris, 1903)

G. Gurvitch, *Essais de Sociologie* (Paris, 1939)

J. Wellhausen, *Reste des arabischen Heidentums* (Berlin, 2nd Edition, 1897)

J. de Maistre, *Traité sur les sacrifices* (Lyon, 12th Edition, 1881)

W. Robertson Smith, *Religion of the Semites* (New York: Meridian Press, 1957)

*The only changes made in the original bibliography have been the substitution of English translations, where such were known to exist. The item order tends to follow the textual references. M. B.

Encyclopaedia of Religion and Ethics (New York: Scribner, 1908–27)

H. Hubert & M. Mauss, "Essai sur la nature et la function du sacrifice," *Mélanges d'histoire des religions* (Paris, 1909)

R. Hertz, "La Prééminence de la main droite," *Mélanges de sociologie religieuse et de folklore* (Paris, 1928)

M. Granet, *Chinese Civilization* (New York, 1930)

L. Gernet & A. Boulanger, *Le Génie grec dans la religion* (Paris, 1932)

L. Lévy-Bruhl, *Primitive Mentality* (New York, 1923)

————, *How Natives Think* (New York, 1925)

————, *The "Soul" of the Primitive* (New York, 1928)

E. Fehrle, *Die kultische Keuschheit im Altertum* (Giessen, 1910)

G. Glotz, *L'Ordalie dans la Grèce primitive* (Paris, 1904)

M. Leenhardt, *Gens de la Grande Terre* (Paris, 1937)

W. Simpson, *The Buddhist Praying Wheel* (London, 1896)

K. T. Preuss, "Der Ursprung der Religion und der Kunst," *Globus,* *LXXVI* (1904) and *LXXVII* (1905)

E. Durkheim & M. Mauss, "De quelques formes primitives de classification," *Année sociologique,* VI (Paris, 1901–02)

R. Lowie, *Primitive Society* (New York: Liveright, Revised Edition, 1947)

M. Mauss, "Les variations saisonnières des sociétés eskimos, *Année sociologique,* IX (1904–05)

J. R. Swanton, "Social Condition, Beliefs, and Linguistic Relationships of the Tlingit Indians," *Bureau of American Ethnology,* XXVI (1908)

A. Moret & G. Davy, *From Tribe to Empire* (New York, 1926)

B. Spencer & F. J. Gillen, *The Northern Tribes of Central Australia* (London, 1904)

M. Granet, *La Pensée chinoise* (Paris, 1934)

F. R. R. S. Raglan, *The Origins of Religion* (London, 1949)

C. de Krelles-Krang, "L'Origine des interdictions sexuelles," *Revue internationale de Sociologie* (July, 1904)

M. Mauss, "La Religion et les origines du droit penal," *Revue de l'Histoire des Religions* (1897) nos. 1–2

S. R. Steinmetz, *Ethnologische Studien zur ersten Entwickelung der Strafe* (Leyden & Leipsig, 1894)

G. Davy, *La Foi jurée* (Paris, 1922)

H. Webster, *Primitive Secret Societies* (New York, 1908)

F. Boas, "The Social Organization and Secret Societies of the Kwakiutl Indians," *Report of the U.S. National Museum for 1895* (Washington, 1897)

Bibliography [183]

A. E. Crawley, *The Mystic Rose* (London, 1927)

A. M. Hocart, *Kingship* (Oxford, 1927)

C. Levi-Strauss, *Les structures élémentaires de la parenté* (Parish, 1949)

G. Dumézil, "Temps et mythes," *Recherches philosophiques*, V (1935–36)

——, *Le Probleme des Centaures* (Paris, 1929)

——, *Mitra-Varuna* (Paris, 1948)

M. Granet, *Festivals and Songs of Ancient China* (New York, 1932)

A. P. Elkin, "The Secret Life of the Australian Aborigines," *Oceania*, III (1932); "Rock-Paintings of North-West Australia" *Ibid.*, I (1930)

C. Daryll Forde, *Ethnography of the Yuma Indians* (Berkeley, 1931)

L. R. Farnell, *The Cults of the Greek States* (Oxford, 1921)

R. Hertz, "La Representation collective de la mort," *Mélanges de sociologie religieuse et de folklore* (Paris, 1928)

P. de Felice, *Poisons sacrés et ivresses divines* (Paris, 1936)

——, *Foules en délire, ontases collectives* (Paris, 1947)

C. Strehlow, *Die Aranda und Loritja-Stamme in Central-Australia* (Frankfort, 1907–20)

T. G. H. Strehlow, *Aranda Traditions* (Melbourne, 1947)

M. Leenhardt, *Do Kamo, la personne et le mythe dans le monde mélanesien* (Paris, 1947)

G. Bianquis, *Faust à travers quatres siècles* (Paris, 2nd Revised Edition, 1955)

G. G. de Bévotte, *La Legende de don Juan* (Paris, 1911)

R. Caillois, *Le Mythe et l'homme* (Paris, 1938)

W. J. Doheny, ed., *St. Teresa of Avila, Selected Writings* (Milwaukee: Bruce, 1950)

NOTES

1. (Editions Quillet), I, 21–32.

2. *Le sacré de respect, esquisse d'une description du système général des interdits et de son fonctionnement dans certaines des sociétés, dites primitives,* CXX (July–August, 1939), 45–87.

3. (Mexico: Fondo de Cultura Economica, 1942), pp. 163–80.

4. No. 10, pp. 66–67.

5. "Le Jeu comme structure," *Deucalian,* No. 2 (1947), pp. 161–67.

6. The word in the French text is *phratries,* which must be translated as "moieties" in accordance with anthropological usage. M. B.

7. *Jeu des prémices* in the French text. M. B.

8. *Surdité, claudication, cécité* in the French text. M. B.

9. *L'adresse* in the French text. M. B.

10. *Le bon droit* in the French text. M. B.

11. Li-K'uei, a jurist of the Han period, and codifier of Chinese law. In revised form, his code is known as the "Collected Statutes of the Manchu Dynasty." Cf. W. Eberhard, *A History of China* (University of California Press, 1950), p. 80. M. B.

12. *Rester pour haïr* in the original text. M. B.

13. *Totales* in the French text. M. B.

14. This work is, as it can only be, schematic. Moreover, my only ambition is to suggest that the problems, such as that of the incest taboo about which so much has been written, can only be properly solved if they are considered as particular instances of a system that embraces the totality of religious taboos in a given society.

15. Cf. E. W. Gifford, *Miwok Moieties,* "University of California Publications," XII (1916), 139–194, and *Clans and Moieties in Southern California, idem,* XIV (1918). 155–219. This particular case enables one to understand how animal heraldry can survive separately after the cosmic principle to which it is bound has lost all social significance.

16. *Nail de la composition* in the French text. *"Composition"* is italicized by Caillois. M. B.

17. August Hardeland, *Versuch Einer Grammatik der Dayakschen Sprache* (Amsterdam: F. Muller, 1858).

18. The potlatch. M. B.

19. "In Greek religion, a personification of compelling necessity, or ultimate fate, to which even the Gods must yield." Cf. Merriam Webster, *Webster's New International Dictionary* (2nd Edition, Unabridged; (Springfield, Mass.: G. & C Merriam Co., 1952), p. 95. M. B.

20. Etienne de La Boétie, French writer, 1530–1568. M. B.

21. The Nubians (*NOUBA* in the French text) may also refer to a contemporary culture, the NUBA, a Negro tribe located in South Kordofan, and related to the Nubians. M. B.

22. It is pointless to emphasize that this theory of the festival is far from an exhaustive account of its different aspects. In particular, it would have to be correlated with a theory of sacrifice. In fact, the sacrificial victim seems to be a kind of privileged character at the festival. It is akin to the inner mechanism that sums it up and gives it meaning. They seem united in the same relationship as soul and body. For want of being able to stress this intimate connection (a choice had to be made), I tried to indicate the sacrificial atmosphere of the festival in the hope that it would thus become meaningful to the reader, just as the dual dialectic of the festival reproduces the dialectic of sacrifice.

23. *Use* in the French text. M. B.

24. Among ethnographers of Australia, this primordial age is referred to as "dream-time." Cf. Alan Marshall, *People of the Dream-Time* (Melbourne, Australia: F. W. Cheshire, 1952). M. B.

25. This is the trickster described by Anglo-Saxon ethnographers (cf. Appendix II).

26. In Greek *Kronos,* a titan who was the son of Uranus and Gaea. He was the God of harvests whom the Romans identified with Saturn. M. B.

27. Madía or Mádo cult (instead of *majo* in the French text). Cf. Gunnar Landtman, *The Kiwai Papuans of British New Guinea* (London: Macmillan, 1927), pp. 408–14ff. M. B.

28. Gaspard de Coligini, French Huguenot, 1519–1572. M. B.

29. A festival like the Roman Saturnalia, in which a slave took the king's role, and later was scourged and executed. Cf. James G. Frazer, *The Golden Bough* (London: Macmillan, 1925), IV, 113ff. and IX, 354ff. M. B.

30. See Appendix III, *War and the Sacred.*

31. The facts, without exception, are drawn from the excellent monograph by Henri A. Junod, *Moeurs et coutumes des Bantous* (Paris:

Payot Editions, 1936). References to this work are always indicated in parentheses, the volume in Roman and the page in Arabic numerals.

32. Here is confirmed the principle of the Polynesian system of purification. At Tonga, the sinner is freed of his defilement by the touch of the chief, whose sanctity, stronger than the defilement, can absorb and neutralize it without danger.

33. This necessity, before returning to the village, of having sexual intercourse with a stranger to whom the previously contracted defilement is passed on is not peculiar to the Bantu. It is also encountered among the Zulu for the purification of the warrior he has slain. After a bath in running water, and various related rites, he starts for the village, watching for any strange woman that passes. He must have sexual relations with a woman not of his tribe in order to be able to take his place in the kraal. Otherwise, he would have continued living in the brush (A. T. Bryant, *A Zulu-English Dictionary*, p. 549). Among the tribes of Northern Rhodesia, a woman who has had a miscarriage, being extremely impure, lives in isolation and cannot resume her place in the village and sexual relations with her husband until she has had them with another man (E. W. Smith and A. M. Dale, *The Ila-Speaking Peoples of Northern Rhodesia*, I, 234–35 and II, 6). Cf. L. Lévy-Bruhl, *Le surnaturel et la nature dans la mentalité primitive* (Paris: 1931), pp. 350 and 399.

34. Actually, this concerns only sexual intercourse among married people, which alone is endowed with importance and power by the society. In fact, the sex practices of youths are not the same. They are deprived of all efficacy and are only games, incapable of the least repercussion upon the course of nature and the fortunes of the community.

35. Among the Kiwai of Papua, the energy derived from sexual intercourse is used for the growth of palm trees on the plantations. But at certain times, they have recourse to very small children. This takes place when it is a question of slowing rather than activating the forces of the vegetable kingdom, for it is considered that if it were possible for children to have sexual intercourse, it would be catastrophic for the harvest (G. Landtman, *The Kiwai Papuans*, p. 68). Among the same people, a woman who has recently had sex relations must not visit a sick person, for he would die. These taboos are widely diffused. Lévy-Bruhl has assembled many similar instances (*Le surnaturel* . . . , pp. 368–70). He has very properly included the cases in which the evil influence is caused by anger, quarreling, envy, etc. (*ibid.*, pp. 189–98). These are in fact emotions or acts that emanate heat just as the sex act and stimulate, by contagion and sympathy, the action of malignant

powers. Nothing is clearer in this respect than the taboo against argument at the harvesting of palm wine at Lebak (*ibid.*, p. 46). It is motivated by the idea that a troubled and agitated spirit will get into the palm wine.

36. While Caillois cites the Spanish translation of Huizinga's work (Mexico: *Fondo de Cultura Económica*, 1943); the English translation (New York: Roy Publishers, 1950) is the present reference. M. B.

37. *Ibid.*, p. 13. Compare the definition of Emile Benveniste: Play is "every regulated activity, which is an end in itself, and does not aim at any practical modification of reality" ("Le jeu comme structure," *Deucalion*, No. 2 [Paris, 1947] p. 161). The documentation with which the author makes his definition clearer, draws it still closer to Huizinga's definition: (1) Play is "an activity that takes place in the world but ignores the reality-principle, because the latter is deliberately viewed as an abstraction." (2) Play does not serve any practical purpose, seeming like a "cluster of forms, the purpose of which cannot be oriented to anything useful." (3) Play "has to unfold within strict limits and conditions, and constitutes a closed universe." By these varied traits, concludes Beveniste, "play is separated from reality, in which human desire, slave to utility, is completely in conflict with accident, incoherence, and arbitrariness, where nothing runs its predicted course, or according to accepted rules. . . ." It must be noted that Benveniste, like Huizinga, has tended to neglect games of chance, which almost always are played for money and have some impact upon reality because the player is enriched or ruined, to the degree that on occasion honor compels him to commit suicide. I maintain that money is sacred, for the miser as well as the gambler. But the miser who accumulates it without daring to touch it, worships it, and at the same time he withdraws it from circulation, removing it from any profane use. That is to say, he behaves toward it in terms of "the sacred as respect." The gambler, on the contrary, who continuously risks it, treats it according to the laws of "the sacred as transgression."

38. Huizinga, p. 10.

39. The author finds confirmation for this mainly in a work by the Hungarian writer, Karoly Kerenyi, "Vom Wesen des Festes," *Paideuma, Mitteilungen zur Kulturkunde,* I, Heft 2 (December, 1938).

40. A. E. Jensen, *Beschneidung und Reifezeremonien bei Naturvolkern* (Stuttgart, 1933).

41. Cf. Appendix I, p. 144.

42. "Die Märchen von klugen Rätsellösern," *Folklore Fellows Communications,* No. 73 (Helsinki, 1928).

43. G. Dumézil, *Mythes et Dieux des Germains* (Paris, 1939), pp. 68–72.

44. The "funny man" in the circus. M. B.

45. Huizinga, p. 165. "What must be done and what one earns thereby are questions that, in play, are only posed as an afterthought." This well applies to play, but not to the activities that the author associates with play.

46. Benveniste, from his vantage point, defines play as a "desocializing operation" (*Deucalion*, pp. 164–65). He also recognizes that the sacred is "tension and anguish," and play is "exaltation and deliverance." Going further, he maintains that play is the product of the separation of myth from rite. Deprived of myth, that is, of sacred words that give acts power over reality, "the rite is reduced to a mechanism ruled by acts that are henceforth ineffectual, to a harmless facsimile of the ceremony, to a pure game (*ludus*)." Conversely, myth without rite results in a simple play upon words (*iocus*), without sum or substance, uncertain, insignificant, and merely empty gestures. Then the battle for possession of the sun becomes a football game, and the probative riddle of initiation no more than a pun.

47. Benveniste even furnishes the formula for passing from the sacred to play. "Every coherent and regulated manifestation of collective or individual life is transposable to play when its rational or empirical motivation, that makes it efficacious, is removed" (*ibid.*, p. 166).

48. Cf. E. von Salomon, *Les Reprouvés*, p. 121 (French translation); cf. pp. 72 and 94.

49. E. Jünger, *La Guerre, notre mère* (Paris, 1934), p. 30 (French translation): cf. E. von Salomon, p. 71.

50. J. Romains, *Les Hommes de bonne volonté, XV, Prélude à Verdun* (Paris, 1938), p. 179.

51. J. Goebbels, *Michel, la Destinée d'un Allemand*, cited by O. Scheid, *L'Esprit du III Reich* (Paris, 1936), p. 219.

52. H. de Keyserling, *La Révolution Mondiale* pp. 69–70, 171 (French Translation): *Meditations Sud-Américaines*, pp. 121–22.

53. E. Ludendorff, *Der Totale Krieg* (Munich, 1937), cited by H. Rauschning, *La Révolution du Nihilisme* (Paris, 1939), p. 114 (French Translation).

54. *Ibid.* (Cf. H. Rauschning. *The Revolution of Nihilism* [New York, 1939], p. 126 [English Translation].) M. B.

55. Jünger, p. 30.

56. *Ibid.*, p. 15.

57. Keyserling, *Meditations Sud-Américaines*, p. 67.

INDEX